D0162198

ARCHITECT'S GUIDE TO
Feng Shui
EXPLODING THE MYTH

ARCHITECT'S GUIDE TO

Feng Shui

EXPLODING THE MYTH

BY

CATE BRAMBLE

AMSTERDAM   BOSTON   HEIDELBERG   LONDON
NEW YORK   OXFORD   PARIS   SAN DIEGO
SAN FRANCISCO   SINGAPORE   SYDNEY   TOKYO

Architectural Press
An imprint of Elsevier
Linacre House, Jordan Hill, Oxford OX2 8DP
200 Wheeler Road, Burlington, MA 01803

First published 2003

Copyright © 2003, Cate Bramble. All rights reserved

The right of Cate Bramble to be identified as the author of this work
has been asserted in accordance with the Copyright, Designs and
Patents Act 1988

No part of this publication may be reproduced in any material form
(including photocopying or storing in any medium by electronic means
and whether or not transiently or incidentally to some other use of this
publication) without the written permission of the copyright holder except
in accordance with the provisions of the Copyright, Designs and Patents
Act 1988 or under the terms of a licence issued by the Copyright
Licensing Agency Ltd, 90 Tottenham Court Road, London, England W1T
4LP. Applications for the copyright holder's written permission to
reproduce any part of this publication should be addressed
to the publisher

Permissions may be sought directly from Elsevier's Science and
Technology Rights Department in Oxford, UK: phone: (+44) (0) 1865 843830;
fax: (+44) (0) 1865 853333; e-mail: permissions@elsevier.co.uk. You may
also complete your request on-line via the Elsevier homepage
(http://www.elsevier.com), by selecting 'Customer Support' and then
'Obtaining Permissions'

British Library Cataloguing in Publication Data
A catalogue record for this book is available from the British Library

Library of Congress Cataloguing in Publication Data
A catalogue record for this book is available from the Library of Congress

ISBN 0 7506 56069

For information on all Architectural Press publications
visit our website at www.architecturalpress.com

Typeset by Newgen Imaging Systems (P)Ltd, Chennai, India
Printed and bound in Great Britain by Biddles Ltd, www.biddles.co.uk

Contents

Acknowledgements

I have always relied on the kindness of strangers. This book would be about parrots had I not had the good luck to study with Master Larry Sang and to meet Master Joseph Yu, Joey Yap and Grandmaster Yap Cheng Hai (whose generosity widened my world to include Master Eva Wong, Master Raymond Lo, and many other notables in this global community). I may never be able to thank all of you enough but I will keep trying.

I am also deeply grateful to my friends, most notably Danny Thorn, Elizabeth Moran, Nani Shaked, and Nancy Chen, who supplied endless hours of advice, suggestions, enlightenment, encouragement, and humour. Joey Yap and Grandmaster Yap provided much-needed wisdom. Architects Simona Mainini and David Wong were kind enough to read the manuscript and provide a much-needed reality check. Loraine Scott, I cannot thank you enough for the Mac that I entrusted with my thoughts. It never failed and for that I am glad.

Without the staff at Architectural Press (Katherine, Alison, and Elizabeth) none of this would be. Thank you all.

Foreword

When I first got onto the internet 5 years ago and searched about Feng Shui, I was surprised it appeared that this ancient Chinese practice was quite well received by westerners. However, when I examined the websites and went to the book stores to find out what were available, to my dismay, it was not what Feng Shui was meant to be. I was happy when Cate Bramble's website 'Feng Shui for Dummies' caught my eyes. The articles not only showed that Cate was sincere about learning Feng Shui, she was brave enough to declare war on what was not. She continues to make an effort to fulfill her mission and her website grows to become 'Feng Shui Ultimate Resource' today.

A lot of Feng-Shui practices can be explained in terms of science. A lot of Feng Shui theories will be proved using scientific approach in the future. Although it may take another 1000 years or even longer before scientists can explain why and how Feng Shui works, it should be our target. Therefore, the way to study Feng Shui and other ancient metaphysics is to use a logical system. I am glad that Cate is following this line.

Cate's book is timely as there are people who claim to be practising traditional Feng Shui but they are actually promoting superstition. This gives a bad name to Feng Shui and gives a bad impression to scientists, architects, and interior designers. It is true that there are phenomena that cannot be explained using science. We cannot use this as an excuse to practise something that insults our common sense and logical reasoning. Cate's standpoint is very firm.

I am sure her readers will welcome her effort to dismiss superstition disguised as Feng Shui.

I am sure architects will find traditional Feng-Shui practices reasonable after reading this book. We can expect more and more architects will be interested in designing houses in accordance with Feng Shui principles.

Joseph Yu

Chapter 1

Introduction: global perspective

Macrocosm to microcosm

> *The jewel that we find, we stop and take it*
> *Because we see it; but what we do not see*
> *We tread upon.*

William Shakespeare: Measure for Measure II, 1

Christopher Alexander in *A Pattern Language* (1977) and *The Timeless Way of Building* (1979) says there is only one way to create human structures that express our humanity and aliveness. Perhaps that explains why Benoit Mandelbrot saw fractal structures only in classic architecture.[1] There must be something to an ancient building if it has managed to sustain us for thousands of years and still compels innovative thinkers to return to its fertile roots.

We want to believe that cities developed almost accidentally, according to political and commercial interests. We acquire that idea from our culture, which understands life as linear history against the traditional view of life as cyclical myth.[2] Yet, cities as we understand them are a very recent phenomenon for human communities. The current idea developed from something the Greeks called the *polis* (which functioned like an extended family) but did not form what we would identify as a 'city' before the European Middle Ages. Before then, and all around the world until quite recently, cities were an expression of the sacred.

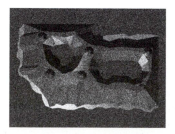

Figure 1.1

Viewed from above, Gaudi's Casa Milo looks as organic and timeless as any natural setting. From a model in DesignWorkshop Lite.

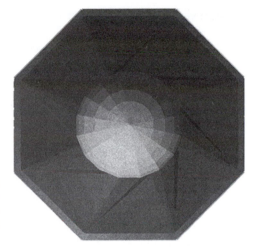

Figure 1.2

The Dome of the Rock provides the squared circle of a traditional building. From a model in DesignWorkshop Lite.

James and Thorpe (1999), in *Ancient Mysteries*, wonder why our ancestors shared the urge to reshape the planet for reasons that do not look quite sane to us. Mound building, straight and wide paths that run for kilometers to nowhere, stone monuments that chart the movements of celestial objects, cities that align to the cardinal directions and whose buildings can be used as astronomical instruments are part of our human heritage. Wheatley (1971), in *The Pivot of the Four Quarters*, showed that urban design expressed in a variety of Asian literature and architecture, and in some nineteenth-century American towns, conveyed the same designs. *What were our ancestors thinking?*

Human urban design in many places and times has conformed to the same mythic vision because it most profoundly expresses what makes us human. The planning of human habitations has generally been meant for a larger spiritual purpose—and generally an unconscious one.[3] Traditional habitation seeks to mirror nature's ways as a form of respect, and human cultures provide mythic justification for these acts. Buildings everywhere used to be imbued

with magic, carefull oriented to the heavens and nearby spiritual features of the land, and integrated with the world at large.

Planetary rotation helped us define cardinal directions which, along with the centre, 'here', assumed importance for humans more than 10000 years ago. Cardinal and intercardinal directions impose cultural structure on nature and serve as a memory aid that strengthens and transmits modes of thought over generations. Humans first mapped the heavens, identified the celestial landscape with land formations, and arranged their dwellings and cities according to the scheme. Settlements were built to invoke these features. Designing on this scheme revealed the underlying movements of the universe.

Myth provides the ultimate technology because it uses our brain and its capacity for memes and memeplexes to encode extremely sophisticated information and transmit it far beyond our own time. A culture's myths make it possible for its members to acknowledge reality (nature). Myth served as the original way to encode traditional knowledge, including the science of a culture.

Petroglyphs at Teotihuacán orient the city on an east–west axis with respect to the sky and can be used for astronomy (one pair of markers indicates the Tropic of Cancer). The *Talmud* says that if a town is to be laid out in a square (which identifies what is made by humans), its sides must correspond to the cardinal directions and align with Ursa Major and Scorpio (*Eruvim* 56a). The practices of *al-qibla*, built into the Ka'aba and all mosques, orient east and west sides to sunrise at the summer solstice and sunset at the winter solstice. The south faces of mosques and the Ka'aba align to the rising of Suhail (Canopus). Spatial configurations like these form part of many cultures' scientific systems, but Westerners often cannot breach their cultural framework and accept this understanding of the world.[4]

Jauch (1973) in *Are Quanta Real?* considered that cyclical movement, a common feature in traditional and mythic thought, helps humans understand the enormity of the universe—including their own insignificance—as well as reality. (Cyclical thought, in Jauch's

Figure 1.3

The Globe Theatre of Elizabethan England features classic shapes aligned for good viewing, and acoustics. Moreover, the bulk of the building lies at the back. From a model in DesignWorkshop Lite.

opinion, is eminently useful today as a heuristic technique simply because it works so well.) Traditional building provides a way for humans to be constantly reminded of their insignificance, just as myths typically celebrate the deeds of those who humble themselves. The mythic model articulates a respectful interaction with nature to draw upon its inspiration and power.

Cosmology and the city

> *The city of Shang was carefully laid out, it is the centre of the four quarters; majestic is its fame, bright is its divine power; in longevity and peace it protects us, the descendants.*
> *From the Book of Odes*

Our architecture and other cultural artefacts unconsciously reflect ideas of cosmic order and embody our values and social reality. They also have the potential to inspire our species' more troublesome instincts to conform to specific customs. Studies indicate that our instinctive urges can be guided merely by the presence and arrangement of nonhuman beings, landscape, and architecture.

To the ancients, subtly persuading humans to be their best meant creating habitations in harmony with nature. The ancients assessed all probable consequences of erecting a structure on the balance of nature and designed for the relationship between a building and the cosmos. Out of Greek geometry a few centuries ago Western culture fashioned the concept of 'sacred geometry' to supply a spiritual plan for monumental architecture.[5] However, thousands of years earlier Chinese culture devised its own system— a radically different approach to addressing the same issues.

Careful planning in traditional building was essential—especially with capital cities, which assumed the responsibility for the welfare of a state. What you see in the planning of a traditional city—and especially in the planning of premodern Chinese cities—flows from what Mircea Eliade identified as the sacred practice of building.[6]

Reality is a function by which humans imitate the celestial archetype

Trinh Xuan Thuan in *Chaos and Harmony* (2001) sees the universe applying certain laws to create diversity. Harmony supplies the pattern and chaos supplies creative freedom. All the high cultures of Asia and most of the high cultures of the premodern world built their cities as a terrestrial celebration of the universe.

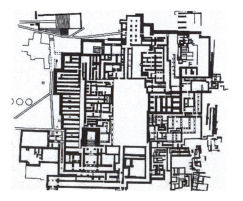

Figure 1.4

A large complex like Knossos follows the classic shapes, but it also brilliantly conveys the genius of the society that constructed it. From a model in DesignWorkshop Lite.

Figure 1.5

The Pantheon complex is aligned symmetrically but follows the patterns humans expect. From a model in DesignWorkshop Lite.

The traditional worldview of Chinese culture supplies a profound cosmology for generating symbolism. A Chinese city was built only after a considerable list of requirements was satisfied. Local influences (*xingqi*), dynamic powers of what an ancient Roman might call the *genius loci* or 'spirit' of a place, were determined before construction in accordance with the shape of local terrain and the stars and planets wheeling overhead. No expense was spared to ensure that the city conformed to traditional design principles. Space–time is paramount in the traditional ideology of Chinese building, which resides in the 'Kaogong ji' (Manual of Crafts) section of the *Zhou li*. The site and date for groundbreaking had to be confirmed by heaven in advance. In the *Book of Odes* one Neolithic ruler consults tortoise shells to obtain information whether a particular area offers the appropriate place and time for construction.

Humans mimic the macrocosm and the microcosm by conducting themselves so that they maintain harmony between the cosmos and their world

All rites used in the founding of settlements and cities seek to bring the human world to life within the cosmic scheme. Determining structural orientation, laying a foundation stone, and performing a sacrifice express the primordial creation of the world.

Orienting a structure to a particular time and place creates a microcosm of a meaningful instant. Founding rites also pull a civic entity from the quantum world (unpredictable, invisible, no direction of time) into the human one (visible, predictable, distinct matter and energy, forward direction of time).

Most traditional African religions promote the idea of harmony between humans, the natural world, and the world that cannot be seen—which, depending on your viewpoint, could be anything from spirits to dark matter, bacteria, and viruses. Daoist thinking consists of working with the planet, even to the point of cultivating 'uselessness' to avoid exploitation. In China, master builders applied the primary scientific theories of Chinese civilization to individual structures. Significant numbers and celestial objects were conveyed in the design of government buildings and humble dwellings,[7] just as Renaissance artists sought to incorporate 'divine proportions' in paintings and monumental architecture. Traditional Korean architects analysed terrain before building so that their structures did not usurp the primacy of nature. They hid or de-emphasized necessary building or engineering devices and accentuated natural features. Building materials were used as if they had appeared naturally.

Reality is achieved by participating in a symbolic centre

For example, the circumpolar constellation Purple Palace (*Zigong*) was the model for the palace in the Ming city of Beijing.[8] The architectural symbolism of the centre validated and demonstrated the power of the emperor who embodied the pole star and the nation's subservience to the forces of nature.

Orientation techniques for defining sacred territory in profane space emphasize the cardinal compass directions

Many cultures established cities on cosmology. Traditional people align primary streets to cosmic markers, establish streets on a cosmic grid, and place major gates on the primary axes. An entire city (including the palace and related structures) often aligns with a direction and/or a particular celestial object. A later design could inherited whatever symbolism accumulated over centuries if not millennia. This made it simpler for conquerors to legitimize their rule by utilizing native cosmology and architecture.

Carl Jung thought that four directions were part of human brain functions, because they often appeared in people's dreams when they were stressed. Humans do have an automatic 'direction sense' that provides a frame of reference so that we can orient ('east') ourselves. This innate cognitive map typically provides four directions (back/front, right/left) and includes a form of internal compass that provides awareness of familiar environments. However, it works only if we stay in our home areas. Our cognitive map includes 'gestalt laws' regarding the orientation of buildings to take advantage of solar gain.[9]

Brave new world

It took approximately three centuries of aggressive work to unseat the traditional view of the world as a holistic system—typically known to us as 'paganism' or 'primitive superstition'—and replace it with the rational, Cartesian one. However, a tidal wave of scientific discoveries threatens to resurrect this old worldview—one that many hoped had been relegated to history (or at least restricted to pseudoscientists, *artistes*, and other belittled groups). In a classic case of 'revenge effect' or philosophical hubris,[10] the ancient worldview has been partially reinstated through rational scientific inquiry and romantic popularizers such as Fred Alan Wolf and Fritjof Capra. Evidently, everything is more closely linked than previously

Figure 1.6

The Pentagon conveys classic design in a favoured shape of Vitruvius. Photo from US Department of Defense.

thought, so that the effects of actions are likely to be more widely felt than previously acknowledged.[11] This is a scary thought to people who have not adjusted to ideas of nonlinear systems, quantum mechanics, and chaos theory (sensitivity to initial conditions)—the scientific concepts that overthrew reductionism and renewed interest in the ancient worldview.

Claude Lévi-Strauss anticipated that science would eventually be sophisticated enough to explain the validity of mythological thinking and help us to close the gap between our mindset and the rest of the universe. Science can explain how much of what makes us human is built on metaphors for our experience of the natural world.[12] Now we have a better understanding of why myth cannot and should not be eradicated. It is time to engage the natural world and ancient traditions before they disappear and humanity goes completely insane.

We have met a traditional human—us

Humans are a product of the natural world and our bodies respond favourably to the introduction of natural elements because we are 'hard-wired' that way.

A substantial body of research indicates that human concepts of what Jiahua Wu (1995) calls 'landscape aesthetics' construct the natural world before the Industrial Revolution. Across national, racial, and cultural differences, humans largely tend to choose an unspectacular or even mediocre natural setting over an urban setting devoid of nature. A large and consistent volume of research demonstrates the stress-reducing effects of natural settings and human observation of animals. Other studies conclude that an appreciation of natural pattern, natural beauty, and natural harmony are part of humanity's genetic makeup.

If we succeed in replacing the natural world that shaped us with objects of our own design our entire species is likely to go mad—if we are not nearly there already. Science advises us that the natural world preserves our mental health. That is why pets, ponds, wild animals, and views of parks and waves reduce our blood pressure and lower the production of adrenaline. Contrary to conventional wisdom, crime rates drop when the amount of vegetation around us increases.

Humans associate relaxation and peacefulness with natural settings that include a water feature. We prefer calm water before us to refresh us and to offer a soothing view. We prefer the presence of vegetation and animals in our vicinity, and desire a mountain or other imposing natural feature at our backs. Our early, not-quite-human ancestors also located their settlements this way. We also prefer the mechanics and infrastructure of modern living to be quiet and unobtrusive. Feng shui's ideal conditions for human happiness and well-being are programmed into our genes.

Traditional methods of feng shui supply a creative problem-solving system to analyse the built and natural environments and to better understand and improve the quality of life. This traditional, sustainable philosophy provides time-honoured techniques of environmental protection. On an extremely simplified level, feng shui can be understood as an attempt to re-establish a dialogue between humanity's deepest needs and our long-estranged, much-abused planet.

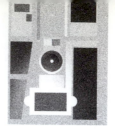

A final note

This book is not designed as self-help for the study of feng shui. You can locate the worthwhile self-help books in Chapter 15, but none can provide instruction on all aspects of authentic feng shui and none can compare to study with a competent instructor. What this book hopes to provide is factual information on aspects of authentic feng shui practise, and suggestions on integrating principles of traditional feng shui into the modern practise of architecture. It hopes to offer a perspective on scientific principles that seem to underpin certain aspects of the traditional practice.

You definitely will not find much 'new age' thinking in these pages because that mindset has nothing to do with feng shui. Traditional feng shui is part of Chinese traditional science (ethnoscience) and follows a long history of interactions and knowledge of the world—empirical knowledge built up over generations and grounded in practical evidence.[13] It also emphasizes attachment to place. Anything 'new age' (and especially 'new age' feng shui which I call McFengshui) is just nineteenth-century spiritual and occult ideology in posh packaging.[14] Moreover, 'new age' feng shui has no basis in traditional science, legitimate science, or traditional practices.

If feng shui is going to work in the modern world it has to meet the world's criteria. Let us see if it can.

Notes

[1] Research based on aerial photos of traditional settlements in west and central Africa shows that they tend to have a fractal structure (scaling in street branching, recursive rectangular enclosures, circles of circular dwellings, etc.). These are the result of intentional designs and are found in other areas of African material culture.

[2] Myth, in one anthropologist's view, creates the illusion that humans can control and completely understand the universe.

[3] In the prevailing scientific view, humans process visual information outside their focus of attention; some say this happens automatically (Craven, 2002). Most of what happens within us is beyond our perceptual range. Conscious and unconscious interpretations and motives often conflict. People around us generally know better about what is going on inside us than we do, based on their observations of our behaviour (Wilson, 2002).

[4] See Joseph (1991) and Ascher (2002).

[5] Geometry is found in all buildings but Chinese geometry is not Western geometry—no Chinese noun corresponds to 'triangle' for example. In Chinese geometry, straight lines are water, pointed shapes are fire, round shapes are soil/earth, curved shapes are wood, and square shapes are metal.

[6] See Eliade (1991).

[7] Traditionally, one part of an imperial palace in a capital was named *Taiji*, after the pole star. Beijing is sometimes known as *Zijin Cheng*, the Polar Forbidden City.

[8] *Ziwei yuan* (Purple Court) consists of several stars in the constellation Westerners know as Draco. The cosmology behind Chinese use of the circumpolar stars is very ancient.

[9] See Johnsson (2002, pp. 316–17).

[10] The *revenge effect*, much like the Law of Unintended Consequences, is defined as the situation when new structures, devices, and organisms react with real people and real creatures in real situations in ways that were not foreseen or intended. These are considered system effects and they can be tightly or loosely coupled. Complexity makes it difficult to determine how a system might act. A tightly coupled system can create problems from the beginning. Complexity and tight coupling create a higher potential for new disasters, especially of global proportions.

[11] Species in a variety of habitats have been shown to be generally within three links of one another, with the average number of links between organisms being just two. Few species in a community are four links from each other. This means that every species is ecologically connected to every other species in a community (Dunne et al., 2002; Williams et al., 2002).

[12] See Lakoff and Johnson (1999).

[13] Ethnoscience is the study of interactions and of traditional knowledge of the world. It is based on the work of Harold Conklin among the Hanunoo of the Philippines in the 1950s. Traditional people are generally recognized by science as a potential source of knowledge. Interestingly, Joseph Needham championed the view that feng shui is an ethnoscience, partially on the fact that its principles follow the scientific model and are based on calculations and complex mathematical formulae.

[14] See Krupp (1991, p. 320). 'New age' also draws upon disturbing nineteenth-century cultural themes, along with apocalyptic visions from the Middle Ages (see Goodrick-Clarke, 1992; Cohn, 2001).

Chapter 2

Expert rules

> *If a man climbs a mountain, the oxen below look like sheep and the sheep like hedgehogs.*
> *Yet their real shape is different.*
> *It is a question of the observer's viewpoint.*
>
> *From the Lushi chunqiu*

$\mathcal{T}$ he theories of yin and yang and the five elements (*wuxing*) form the philosophical basis of traditional Chinese science. Professor Liu Yanchi (1998) suggests the best way for a Westerner to appreciate these theories may be to think of them in terms of concepts like systems theory (which blends the study of quantities with the study of form or pattern) and complexity theory (which tries to explain how something might begin from a random or chaotic state and yet produce complex order).[1] Concepts of disorder and randomness—also called *chaos*—are included in the study of complex systems. Scientifically, a child's room is not 'a cluttered mess', it is a 'complex environment' (*complex* can refer to deliberately created anarchy and to random messiness).

The theories of yin and yang and the five elements also contain the concept of resonance, *ganying*, which is something like the so-called butterfly effect.[2] Neils Bohr sounded like a Daoist when he said that one cannot assume the universe has separate and independent units. In Chinese thinking, the Dao or *Naturally So* embraces and underlies all things, and a disturbance in one area of a system resonates in another. Science shows us this side of the world. People used to think elephants were psychic or something because of their 'uncanny' abilities to find one another over long distances—now we know they communicate infrasonically.[3] Bacteria 'talk' through the air and they transmit information that apparently confers antibiotic resistance.[4] Microbes and marine algae seemingly use clouds to further their own ends and may in fact control our planet's climate.[5]

In the traditional mind, activity and anomalies in the sky connect to events on Earth—this can be broadly interpreted as the earliest understanding of space weather (see Chapter 3). Ancient Greeks thought that celestial bodies actually changed the Earth, while Babylonians and Chinese believed that there was only a correspondence. A Babylonian textbook for celestial forecasters explained that aerial phenomena, like terrestrial phenomena, provide 'signals' for us. People heeded these 'signals' to understand local manifestations of cosmic energy.

Yin yang theory

> *[The natural] laws are not forces external to things, but represent the harmony of movement immanent in them.*
>
> *An excerpt from the Yi jing*

This theory uses an explanation of motion and changes in nature as its foundation. It is used with its corollary *wuxing* (five-element theory) in understanding and interpreting nature with the stated goal of harmonization. Yin yang theory, categorized by some as the ancients' understanding of fractals and complexity theory, and *wuxing* provide ecological techniques for approaching and appreciating nature.

Professor Liu Yanchi characterized the relationship of yin and yang of the following aspects:

- *Opposition*. Yin and yang consist of two stages of a cyclical, even wavelike, continually changing relationship; the terms explain the intrinsic contradictions of natural objects or phenomena.
- *Interdependence and intertransformation*. Yin and yang are not independent because they can change into each other. This is a difficult concept for Westerners, whose thinking typically oscillates between *is* and *is not*. In Chinese science, just as in Western complexity theory, phenomena are more readily accepted as inherently paradoxical.[6]
- *Dynamic balance*. The qualities of yin and yang counter and complement because they exist in oscillating flux.[7] This tension of opposites expresses as unity—the *Taiji* or Supreme Ultimate, which is both first and last (see Figure 2.1)—and creates a potential that might manifest energy at any time.[8]

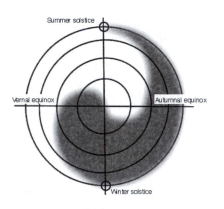

Summer solstice

Vernal equinox

Autumnal equinox

Winter solstice

Figure 2.1

The *Taiji* (Supreme Ultimate), constructed astronomically using a gnomon.

In our universe of constant change there is the *Taiji*, the centre as Dao, and zero, a unified representation of *Liang Yi*, the two primal energies (yin and yang, which suggest that the universe is inherently female because its primary representation is 'cracked in two'). *Taiji* also identifies the circumpolar region.[9] The Taiji evolved into four images, the *si-xiang* that refer to four original constellations (dragon, tiger, turtle, and bird) divided along the celestial equator to indicate astronomical markers (two solstices and two equinoxes).[10] These four images, in turn, evolved into eight elemental trigrams to represent all cosmic and physical conditions affecting living beings and also to identify the winds and directions.[11] From earliest times the eight symbols or *bagua* have been associated with astronomical and topographical features, while the number five at the centre preserved the original astronomical meaning.

Phenomena can be defined in yin yang theory as gradients on a scale of complete yin and yang. There are also opposing states of accumulation—yang for lighter things, yin for heavier things. Yang expands and rises, creates and activates. At its purest and most rarefied, yang is entirely immaterial and consists of pure energy. Yin condenses and materializes, contracts and descends. Yin at its

Figure 2.2

Evolution of yin and yang, after Shao Yong. *Daiyang* (old, stable yang) and *Xiaoyin* (young, changing yin) are summer solstice and spring equinox, respectively. *Daiyin* (old, stable yin) and *Xiaoyang* (young, changing yang) are winter solstice and autumnal equinox, respectively. The original, 'changeable' trigrams are the so-called East Group of Kan and Xun, Li and Zhen. The 'stable' trigrams are the West Group of Kun and Gen, Dui and Qian.

most coarse and dense is matter. One famous representation of yin–yang generation is shown in Figure 2.2.

Westerners see *matter* and *energy* in terms of the first law of thermodynamics, with energy constantly transforming to matter and vice versa. Substitute *yang* for 'energy' and *yin* for 'matter' and you have a basic understanding of yin yang theory. Table 2.1 describes some of the many qualitative aspects of yin yang theory.

Wuxing (five element theory)

Try to explain *wuxing* to Westerners and you invariably run into the five Greek elements, which were in fact material substances—Earth, air, fire, water, and quintessence. (Unfortunately, the Greeks did not know about chemical elements; they also did not know that

Table 2.1

Some qualitative aspects of yin and yang

Qualities of yang	Qualities of yin
Above	Below
Intensity	Persistence
Back side	Front side
Bright	Dark
Confucianism	Daoism
Day	Night
Dry	Wet
East	West
Expand	Contract
Fast	Slow
Features of landscape	Retained water
Fire	Water
Fly	Walk
Function	Structure
Generate	Grow
Hard	Soft
Immaterial	Material
Intentionality	Passivity
Left	Right
Noisy	Quiet
Noon	Midnight
North of the ecliptic	South of the ecliptic
Outside	Inside
Produce energy	Produce form
Qi[1]	Fluids
Rapid	Gradual, lingering
Restive	Still
Rise	Descend
Round	Flat
Smooth	Rough
South	North
Summer solstice	Winter solstice
Sun	Moon
Time	Space

[1] *Qi* (in earlier systems rendered *ch'i*) implies many things to Westerners—most of them inappropriate. (Using the word 'energy' to mean *qi* can be misleading; identifying *qi* as 'the Force' as in *Star Wars* is ludicrous.) *Qi* can refer to the activity of life (and to the traditional mind life is an aspect of being). It can also refer to mood or to an active influence (perhaps something auditory, atmospheric, bacterial, viral, or chemical). In Chinese science, numbers (*shu*) along with principles (*li*) and *qi* describe and direct how nature functions.

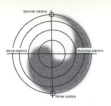

atoms do not exhibit the geometrical structures they assigned to them.) *Wuxing* does not express this thinking at all. The term actually identifies processes, qualities, and phases of cycles, inherent capabilities, or changing phenomena. At its most basic, according to Professor Liu, *wuxing* explains how systems (objects or phenomena) contain structural qualities that interact with each other and how these interactions produce outcomes in predictable patterns. A scientist can describe the cycle of life on Earth in a wavelike motion according to *wuxing* as living creatures coming out of rocks and going back into rocks, and explain H_2O in 'phases' of water, steam, and ice.

Wuxing provides a framework for viewing the components of any system, their relationship, and the pattern of motion based on their interaction. With *wuxing* we can employ analogy to understand the world. We can use the obvious qualities of one system to describe unknown and/or unspecified qualities of another. We can explain the behaviour of objects and phenomena in nature, including cycles of change over time.

The ancients selected common natural materials—wood, fire, Earth, metal, and water[12]—to characterize the behaviour of all natural objects and phenomena. Each symbol represents an analogy with its own rules for actions and results of movement for any phenomenon or object. Positive outcomes occur in *xiang sheng* (mutual production, the order of wood–fire–soil–metal–water) and negative outcomes occur in *xiang ke* (mutual destruction, the order of metal–wood–soil–water–fire). Table 2.2 depicts one of innumerable Chinese 'analogy maps' of five element theory.

Time and space

Perhaps it was during the period of the Yin (Shang) (fourteenth to eleventh centuries BCE) that astronomers divided the celestial circle into the four 'palaces' (animals) consisting of four wedges oriented to the cardinal points—the shape of the character *ya*.[13] After all, the Shang believed their world was shaped like a *ya*. In Chinese thought, connecting the four points within the celestial

Table 2.2

A Chinese analogy map of five element theory

	Wood/vegetation	Fire	Earth/soil	Metal	Water
Earthly branches [1]	Yin, Mao	Si, Wu	Four seasons	Shen, You	Hai, Zi
Seasonal marker [2]	Spring equinox	Summer solstice	Between	Autumnal equinox	Winter solstice
Colour	Bluegreen	Red	Yellow	White, metallic	Black, plum-black
Constellation [3]	Bluegreen dragon, *Canglong*	Red bird, *Zhuque*	Celestial north pole, *Beiji*	White tiger, *Baihu*	Mysterious Turtle-warrior, *Xuanwu* [4]
Compass point [5]	East	South	Centre (or 'here')	West	North
Lunar lodges (*xiu*) [6]	Jue, Kang, Di, Fang, Xin, Wei, Ji	Donjing, Yugui, Liu, Qixing, Zhang, Yi, Zhen		Kui, Lou, Wei, Mao, Bi, Zixi, Shen	Nandou, Niu, Xunu, Xu, Wei, Yingshi, Dongbi [7]
Organ	Liver	Heart	Spleen	Lung	Kidney
Planet	Year Star, *Sui* (Jupiter)	Sparkling Deluder, *Ronghuo* (Mars)	Quelling Star, *Zheng* (Saturn)	Great White, *Tai bai* or Executioner's Star (Venus)	Chronograph Star, *Chen* (Mercury)
Process/activity	Increasing yang, realized wood	Maximum yang, realized fire	Potential and realized Earth/soil	Increasing yin, realized metal	Maximum yin, realized water
Celestial stems [8]	Jia, Yi	Bing, Ding	Wu, Chi	Geng, Xin	Ren, Gui
Time	Sunrise	Noon	Between	Sunset	Midnight
Weather (and pathogenic factors)	Windy	Hot	Humid	Dry	Cold
Wind	Bright abundance, *Mingshu*	Brilliant, *Jing*		Gate of Heaven, *Changhe*	Broad dimness, *Guangmo*
Yin yang theory	Yang within yin	Yang within yang	Buffer or neutral	Yin within yang	Yin within yin

¹ Twelve branches each indicate a month of the year and each 'month' marks an Earth-year in the orbit of Jupiter (rounded to 12 years from an actual 11.86 years) and the movement of *Taisui*, also known as *Daiyin*. Movements of *Dayin/Taisui* were indicated on the *shi*, a Qin-era board tentatively identified as the original feng-shui instrument. *Dayin* calculations were part of military forecasting, according to the *Xingde* texts unearthed at Mawangdui, and *Dayin* (as *Taisui*) is still calculated in feng shui. The branches are also part of the 24 Mountains sequence (see Chapter 3). Five multiples of 12 branches indicate the Jupiter cycle of grand conjunctions with Saturn ($5 \times 12 = 60$). Taisui is the 'minister of time' with a staff of 120; in an unpromising aspect it harms homes and anyone on a thoroughfare.

² These indicate the yang area of Earth (above the ecliptic); obviously, the seasons would be reversed for the yin area (below the ecliptic) but no other designations change—whether above or below the ecliptic we live on the same planet and everyone experiences days of equal length at the equinoxes.

³ In 1875, Gustav Schlegel published *Uranographie Chinoise* and the stunning hypothesis that some Chinese constellations can be dated to 15 600 BCE. Julius Staal translated Schlegel's book and employed a Zeiss planetarium projector to reproduce Schlegel's work. Staal published his findings in *Stars of Jade* (1984). Unfortunately, his work has not received a great deal of attention. Recent analyses of 'star maps' depicted in some grottos at Lascaux suggest that Schlegel's hypothesis should be fully investigated. Supposedly, the 'large hall' contains information on a new year celebrated at the autumnal equinox. The calendar used by the people who created the works in Lascaux may have collated the great solar year (18 years $\times 3 = 54$ years) and the lunar year ($18 + 19 + 19 = 56$ years).

⁴ In some representations this animal embraces a snake, which should instead be interpreted as a dragon. *Xiu* sector Ji of the dragon contains an ancient constellation known as *Bie* (Turtle), the ancient version of Xuanwu (*Corona Australis*, near the end of Scorpio). *Tengshe*, the snake of heaven and the awakening serpent, is part of Xuanwu (the Western constellation of *alpha Lacertae*). This turtle also echoes Ao the great sea turtle whose legs were used by the great goddess Nu Gua to support the world after the tilting of the Earth's axis. Bie's shell has the markings of constellations (the bagua); his head is snake-shaped and his neck is dragon-shaped. Turtle and snake at north found their way into the *Amritamanthana* as Kashyapa, the celestial pivot.

⁵ In the ninefold scheme of feng shui, the nine fields consist of a circle surrounded by eight wedges extending in eight directions. This delineation is made by arcs whose midpoints correspond to cardinal and intercardinal directions. 'North' is 45° on either side of celestial north and the 'northern sector' is 22.5° on either side of celestial north (Major, 1993, pp. 36–8).

⁶ These analogies reflect the sky in the Han era. Around 2300 BCE, the time of Yao according to the 'Yaodian' section in the *Book of Documents*, the seasonal indicators that functioned as cardinal directions (*Mao, Xu, Niao, and Huo*) were the same but fell in different times due to the effects of precession, which moves the stars 1° in 77.3 years. Huo (Antares) appearing above the eastern horizon at dusk heralded spring in the Yin (Shang) period.

⁷ *Dongbi* and *Yingshi* form what Westerners call the Square of Pegasus.

⁸ Ten stems have been used since Shang kings instituted a 10-day week (10 suns) and 30-day month (10 suns appearing three times a month). In Yangshao culture, a three-legged bird was identified with the number 3, the quality of yang and the sun; a crow or raven in a circle was identified as the sun. The suns were black birds and the ancestor of the Shang, Black King, is depicted as a beaked head and one large foot, or a figure in a crouching position. A few thousand years before Greek astronomy, Chinese observed sunspots (poetically known as 'the three-legged crow of the sun') through smoky rock crystals and semitransparent jade. Lenses ground from rock crystal have been found and dated to 2300 BCE (the time of Yao).

circle created the equinoctial cross or *ya-xing*. The lower shell of a turtle (plastron) that was used for divination also symbolized the *ya-xing*. *Sifang*, four directions, consisted of four mythical lands where winds originated; they surrounded a central square.[14] The *ya-xing* as mandala inside the celestial circle also appears in ancient Egypt as part of the hieroglyph for 'the black (fertile) land' or *Kemit*, as the nation was then called.

A squared circle or *fang yuan* represents the union of heaven and Earth, the primary Chinese mandala *tian-yuan di-fang*—heaven as round (natural world) and Earth as square (human experience and concepts of order).[15] Although *tian-yuan di-fang* is visible in the architecture of the Altar and Temple of Heaven at Beijing, it is also built into sites of Hongshan culture at Dongshanzui, and at Niuheliang where the southern end of the complex features a round altar like the Temple of Heaven.[16] A rectangular building at the north end of the Niuheliang complex reminded excavating archaeologists of the Qinian Temple, one of the first buildings constructed at the Temple of Heaven.[17]

Chinese traditional science established directions on the assumption that one faced south (the direction of yang, heaven and 'top') and kept one's back to the north (the direction of yin, Earth and 'bottom').[18] The left was identified with east and sunrise (yang) and the right was identified with west and sunset (yin). In the Northern Hemisphere when one faces south and observes the sun it apparently moves 'clockwise' (where we get the term, actually),[19] which is one reason why the Taiji turns 'clockwise' with the white (yang part) up and the black (yin part) down.

Things are looking up

Archaeology indicates that, from at least the Neolithic, Chinese thinking encompassed a spatial organization with heaven above, humanity in the middle, and Earth below. Space itself was represented as a cube with six coordinates (cardinal or intercardinal directions plus up and down), and indicated valuation in terms of yin (square) and yang (round).

Figure 2.3
Yangshao chieftain's grave with the dragon and tiger.

Analysing positions in space-time was of paramount importance to officials in premodern China. They sited buildings according to astronomical phenomena. At the close of the second millennium BCE, construction on the capital of Luoyang began when the constellation we call Pegasus was at its zenith. A Yangshao grave (Banpo phase) at Xishuipo near Puyang faces its round side to the south and its square side to the north (see Figure 2.3).[20] This site provides additional physical proof of the antiquity of basic aspects of feng shui. To the west of the dead chief lies a mosaic of the ancient constellation *Baihu* (White Tiger) and to the east lies a mosaic of the constellation *Canglong* (Bluegreen Dragon), both with their backs to the chief. Below the dead man's feet (to the north) lie leg bones and shells that apparently indicate the constellation of *Beidou* (what Westerners call the Plough, Wagon, Big Dipper, and Bear). On all sides except south excavators found the remains of other people.

An old story claims that the ancient method of siting a capital used meridian transits at night to find the cardinal directions. This probably explains why the Shang-era sites align to celestial north of the time they were built.[21]

By employing simple astronomical techniques people determined that solstices and equinoxes marked out a square, which was the 'flat earth',[22] and the heavens were visualised as moving in a circle or on a dome overhead with the pole star as the axis of the universe ('the round heavens'). The *Zhou li* says this enabled specialists to calculate an *axis mundi* (a centre or 'here') personified by the ruler and the pole star: 'the place where Earth and sky meet, where the four seasons merge, where wind and rain are gathered in, and where yin and yang are in harmony'.

The emperor presided over the Middle Kingdom (*Zhongguo*) in the position of the pole star and functioned as the pivot of Chinese civilization. Building customs imbued Chinese capitals and their rulers with spiritual significance. Someone sitting in a house in a neighbourhood of such a city could truly feel they and their nation were at one with the cosmos.

Each month the position of the emperor's throne was determined by the court astronomers, who observed the sun in conjunction with the moon in a *xiu* (lunar lodge) or with a particular star. The ruler varied the direction he faced to the appropriate part of the sky. In the first 3 months of the year he faced east as he presided in the three eastern rooms of a nine-chambered palace called the Ming Tang[23]—first northeast, then centre-east, and then southeast (see Figure 2.4). In the first moon of summer the emperor faced south as he resided in the southeast room. By facing south his spleen was to the left (east), his lungs in front (south), his liver at right (west), his kidneys behind (north), and his heart at the centre of the Middle Kingdom.

In this system each season was assigned a number (see Figure 2.5). The number of spring is eight ($5 + 3$, because the 5 of soil is associated with all four seasons, and 3 is the number of the wood element). It is displayed in the bottom-left corner of the Luoshu magic square. The number of summer is 7 ($5 + 2$) and the number

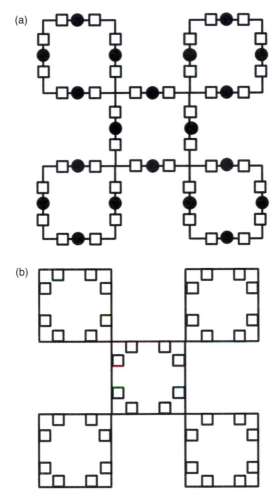

Figure 2.4

(a) A representation of a Ming Tang, after Dai Jen. This diagram could be applied to buildings or large areas of land. In this case, the small squares represent windows and the dark circles represent households. (b) Representation of a Ming Tang in the Zhou period. The drawing represents a plan of households (smaller squares), which typically would be surrounded by a realistic drawing of rammed-earth walls and towers. During the Zhou period a Ming Tang consisted of five squares. During the Qin period the Ming Tang expanded to nine squares.

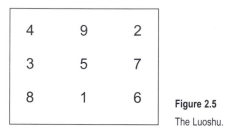

4	9	2
3	5	7
8	1	6

Figure 2.5
The Luoshu.

of autumn is 9 (5 + 4), displayed at the top middle; the number of winter is 6 (5 + 1), which is displayed in the bottom-right corner. The numbers shift as the months progress. The Luoshu in one sense represents the daily circle of the sun envisioned by Neolithic (and possibly earlier) astronomers, the seasonal cycle of nature, the process of growth and decay. The sequence of symbols (trigrams) built into the diagram mark the world changing from winter/sleep/death (Kan) to conception (Gen), birth (Zhen), adulthood to midlife (Kun), and old age (Qian).

Notice that the yin (even) numbers displayed at the corners and the yang (odd) numbers form the *ya* character. A much later interpretation regarding the construction of the Luoshu was that it was a 'calculation of nine halls', which could have any number of levels of significance.[24] The diagram contains (among other things) nine 'star-gods', nine provinces and their emblematic cauldrons, nine 'floating stars', plus nine ritual steps in the pattern of Beidou—used to stop floods and avert evil—known as the *Yubu* or 'steps' of Yu.

The Luoshu also shows agreement with ancient emblems of Sirius and the planet Venus (both assigned the value of 15 in ancient Western Asia), which gave rise to the so-called 'sigil of Saturn'.[25] The *kamea* (amulet) of the sigil is the Luoshu, also known as the magic square of Huangdi the Yellow Emperor—and the gematria equivalent of the shortened form of the Tetragrammaton.[26] Rotate the sigil of Saturn 90° to reveal the cone of precession (the wobble of Earth's axis displayed as a cone) and the seven sefirot of the *Sefer Yetzirah*. The Luoshu also indicates the kabbalistic cube of space with Shabtai (the Hebrew version of Saturn; *Huangdi* to Chinese), the transmitter of mysteries, at its centre. The Luoshu found its way from China (through Jewish and Muslim sources) to medieval Christian Europe as a charm on dinner plates to avert plague.[27]

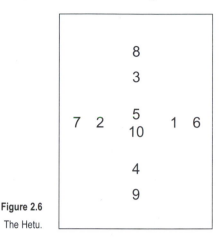

Figure 2.6

The Hetu.

In the Hetu, the numbers 1 through 10 are arranged to pair an odd number with an even number so that 5 and 10 are at the centre (see Figure 2.6). Odd numbers add to 25, even numbers add to 30, and all numbers added together total 55.

In legend, the Hetu discovered by Fuxi came from the Yellow River via a 'horse' (synechedoche for dragon) and was traditionally written in red. Along with red, white, and black, green was used to code star systems on Chinese star maps, which used dark circles and light circles connected by lines to indicate constellations. The Luoshu 'map' is traditionally written in green.

Notes

[1] The *Dao de jing* says that when people discovered what Dao was they laughed at it. Evidently there is no understanding of Dao without laughter. Whether it is a laugh of 'No *really*!' or 'Of course!' is not specified.

[2] Generally attributed to Edward Lorentz, the butterfly effect seeks to explain how seemingly insignificant acts contain far-reaching consequences (provided that certain conditions exist for sensitivity to small perturbations). However, there is an issue of scale: in many cases when such special conditions exist, they are sensitive to a *variety* of possible small disturbances. Lots of butterflies would be needed to influence the weather—or perhaps a few elephants would be sufficient, as these large organic gardeners create ecotones and other microclimates.

[3] See Payne (1998). The same communication method is used by giraffes (see Sherr, 1997).

[4] See Heal and Parsons (2002).

[5] See Hamilton and Lenton (1998).

[6] Evidently paradox constitutes the original conceptual framework for human belief systems (Berman, 2000).

[7] The *Huainanzi* says that yang is born at Zi and yin is born at Wu. *Xiu* sector Zi contains the winter solstice. It is identified with north and located at a point on the celestial circle equal to the midpoint of the northern edge of flat, square 'earth' on a line that connects the points at northwest and northeast on the celestial circle. This excerpt from a Han-period book evokes the traditional explanation of the origins of the Taiji in ancient astronomy. The contrasting light and dark portions on Figure 2.7 denote seasonal changes.

[8] In the diagram called the Hetu or preheaven sequence it is Qian that begins movement. In the diagram called the Luoshu or postheaven sequence, activity starts with Zhen in the east like a sunrise, which starts the real world in motion. Zhen and Xun symbolize beginnings, Gen and Dui symbolize endings.

[9] *Taiji* refers to the ridgepole of a traditional dwelling, suggests the centre of anything as a pole that functions as a gnomon (*gaitian*), and indicates the pole star. A typical illustration shows the four symbolic animals arranged around the Chinese emperor as the pole star.

[10] This ancient system originally provided five 'palaces' or 'resting places' to organize the heavens, dwellings, and Earth. In the circumpolar region the handle of the Dipper, Beidou, ticks off the seasons like a celestial clock, with the cardinal points indicated by the equinoxes and solstices.

[11] This evolution is read on a trigram from the bottom up: Earth, humanity in the middle, and the cosmos.

[12] Some Chinese natural scientists considered Grain as the sixth element.

[13] The shape also formed the Chinese character representing ceremonial, religious, and divinatory specialists (what Westerners call *magi*) and the mother-ancestor of the Shang.

[14] Square settlements are common in ancient China. For example, the Lingjiatan cultural site (5000 years old) is situated on a north–south axis. The north–central area contains a large square laid in fired brick that features two altars surrounded by graveyards. Large stones were placed in such a way that they may have been used for astronomical functions (Cao, 2000).

[15] Talmudists explained the square as the physical world and the circle as the shifting universe of souls; the *Bahir* says, 'A circle inside a square can move', alluding to the sun generating quarter cycles of time and seasons.

[16] Some experts see the *tian-yuan di-fang* in the symbolism of the *bi* (circular disk) and *cong* (hollow, square tube) unearthed with Neolithic Chinese burials. *Bi* were generally placed on the chests of the dead (and sometimes under them as well), while *cong* might be arranged around the body in the cardinal directions, or pointed at the head.

[17] See An (1991).

[18] A Chinese compass (Luopan) needle apparently points south. However, opposite magnetic poles attract and like magnetic poles repel; the so-called 'south pole' is actually our planet's *north* pole. The names of the poles are conventions for opposite ends of a spin—the end of the spin of an atom of cobalt-60 that flings out the most electrons is what we call 'south'. To avoid confusion, science uses the convention of identifying our planet's north magnetic pole as the South Pole so that what we call the 'south geographic pole' matches what we call the 'south magnetic pole'. Chinese traditional scientists had it right from the beginning, but proved it in the 1950s using the methods of modern science—and earned a Nobel Prize for their efforts (Gardiner, 1978).

[19] Shadows move clockwise in the Northern Hemisphere and move anticlockwise in the Southern Hemisphere. In the Northern Hemisphere, the sun is due south when at its highest point in the sky or when an object casts no noticeable shadow. In the Southern Hemisphere, the same noonday sun indicates due north.

[20] See Dong (2002). Placing burials in buildings was typical of Xinglongwa culture in China's Mongolia Autonomous Region. However, as of now it is not known if the large complex at Chifeng has any astronomical significance. House number 22 may have been the home of the community leader because it is different in size and style (it includes six symmetrical columns) and contained delicate pieces of jade. A total of 150 semisubterranean dwellings (*yaodong*) have been located (August and Hammond, 2002).

[21] Ninety per cent of surveyed Xinglongwa sites are situated on terraces close to the northwest side of a river, on fairly level ground, protected from the wind and facing the sun. Astronomical significance has not been confirmed (Ta La et al. (2002)). Zhaogaobou culture apparently also preferred this siting; the settlements so far unearthed show a preference for the northwest side of a river, or the southeast side.

[22] Strangely, this can be verified astronomically only if one travels far to the north of China.

[23] Ming Tang and its legendary upper storey Lingtai reside in the constellation Leo, as does the ancient presence of the Yellow Dragon (*Xuan Yuan*, the original name of Huangdi).

[24] The implication of nine halls is that this version of a Ming Tang dates from the Qin period.

[25] The 'sigil of Saturn' is actually the symbol of the planet's demon, Zazel.

[26] The traditional dates for the reign of the Yellow Emperor (2697–2597 BCE) roughly correspond to Phase II of Wayland's Smithy in the UK. *Gematria* is mathematical information in a poetic form.

[27] For more mathematical history of this magic square see Joseph, pp. 148–56.

The Artificial Sphere

Chapter 3

Protoscientific and pseudoscientific conventions

rchitects have to live down the stereotype of the architect-hero in Ayn Rand's *The Fountainhead*. Feng shui suffers the stereotypes of 'geomancy',[1] superstition, and pseudoscience—never mind that feng shui was the original method of measuring local bioclimatic conditions.

A willing suspension of disbelief?

'Science' consists of any attempt by members of a culture to create a system that makes their observations of nature understandable. Humans have always noticed patterns in nature: night and day, tides and lunar cycles, the changing seasons, animal and plant life cycles. Pattern recognition contains meaning for us because cycles and steady states are important for our existence. In fact, our ability to recognize patterns supplies our basic notions of intuition.

Authentic feng shui is typically identified as a protoscience or an ethnoscience.[2] It allows the data to speak for themselves—which means that people do not analyse a structure with any precon-ceived ideas about the way things ought to be. Feng shui applies expert rules (see Chapter 2) and provides an abundance of formulae that assign numeric values to everything from compass readings to time periods (see Chapter 4).

Feng shui 'lite' (which I call *McFengshui*) is more of a lifestyle issue or a pseudoscience, which replaces scientific uncertainty with views based on political or religious beliefs and seeks to provide answers for everything. McFengshui uses no instrumentation and cannot collect quantitative data. This belief system is forced to rely on its concepts such as 'clutter' and the idea of 'corners' needing 'activation'.

The forecast

Numbers manipulated and interpreted according to their qualities (*numerology*) form the core of many ancient number systems.

This type of mathematics uses speculative and/or symbolic meanings of numbers to understand the structure of the world. (Numbers, mathematics, and astronomy developed from each other.) Numbers formed the basis of Chinese forecasting—more colourfully known as *divination*—from at least the Yin (Shang) period (fourteenth to eleventh centuries BCE). In ancient Chinese culture, writing was the key to predictive power because knowledge from the past (such as histories) linked the living and the dead. Chinese corresponded with the world through events, numbers, and their symbolism. Numbers were associated with cryptographic mathematics in the Hetu (River Chart) and Luoshu (Lo River Writing), which represented models of the world and conveyed an inner meaning for life (see Figure 3.1).

Figure 3.1

An historic rendering of the equator, tropics, polar circles, and ecliptic. Treasures of the NOAA Library Collection. Archival photograph by Sean Linehan, NOS, NGS.

In a technique Joseph Needham called 'threes and sevens riding the qi', 60 divisions with 24 azimuthal compass points and 36 divisions with odd numbers, it is obvious that the numbers relate to astronomy. Heaven's 7 and Earth's 3 refer to Hetu numbers (7 = fire and 3 = wood, 7 + 3 = 10). Ten is the central number of the Hetu and symbolizes Dao as present.

Divination in modern life

> *Nuclear physics is full of uncertainties and probabilities, yet the bombs still kill you.*
>
> Jim Washburn, California journalist

Figure 3.2

A weather divination expert.
National Image Library.

We may scoff at divination but we use it daily. Probably the most famous form of American divination is the annual celebration of Groundhog Day (2 February, known to Europeans as Candlemas). A large, native American rodent (a woodchuck, *Marmota monax*) is used to forecast the weather. According to research on this practice conducted by the US Weather Service, weather divination by groundhog is statistically as reliable as a weather newscaster (see Figure 3.2).

Modern divination does not stop at furry prophets. Women still toss their wedding bouquets for unmarried female guests—a form of spontaneous divination no different than dowsers or people who pick up 'psychic vibrations' from household and personal objects.

If feng shui consists of divination why do scholars prefer to compare Chinese divination to the forecasting methods of an economist or some other boffin? Because we are not talking about foretelling the future (which cannot be done). Chinese divination describes *probabilities*. Consider feng shui an ancestor of complexity theory, which for some assumes the guise of divination.

In complexity theory *forecasting* involves a statement, usually in probabilistic terms, about the future state or properties of a system based on a known past and present. A *conditional forecast* states

in probabilistic terms what the future will be if one follows a particular course of action. A *prediction* is a forecast that states with a high degree of confidence what the future will be. A *scenario* is a forecast that is a hypothesis rather than a formally justified inference from past data. A *forecasting horizon* indicates the length of time ahead of now for which one can make a reasonable forecast. It depends, in general, on available data.

Humans cannot make long-term plans if they cannot predict the outcome. High trust in a forecasting horizon is critical when someone does not have the confidence to proceed. Science yields predictive information (usually through the use of statistics), but every day people face decisions where it is impractical or impossible to gather justification by statistics. They have to base at least part of their choices on unproven beliefs.

People often rely on some form of divination in these situations because it offers a decision-making system within the phase transition space of creative thinking. Divination as a decision-making technique begins with an acceptable level of control and certainty (such as ritual or tradition), proceeds to the far reaches of ideology and vision (including belief systems) right to the border of creative thinking and chaos (ecstatic experience and madness). This is a fairly comprehensive appraisal of human consciousness according to complexity theory.

The recording of sequences of unusual or important events is one of the most enduring forms of divination. Volume after volume of Chinese history offers documented occurrences of strange births, the tracking of natural phenomena, and other data. Chinese governmental planning relied on this method of forecasting for long-range strategy. It is not unreasonable to assume that modern scientific inquiry originated in such forms of divination (Joseph Needham's work considers this very theory).

We rely on this today, but do not think to associate it with divination. For example, the US National Climatic Data Center publishes a monthly publication, *Storm Data*, which contains a by-state and by-date listing of storms and unusual weather occurrences.

The publication provides information on paths of storms plus deaths, injuries, and property damage. It includes a feature on the 'outstanding storms of the month' concerning freak and severe weather events. Cataloguing information and cryptographic mathematics correspond to what is called 'human observer capability' in complexity theory. They also relate to decision-making.

Why would someone practice divination to site a house or a city? Consider how a typical building affects the environment and how such an imposition contains unforeseen risks—the butterfly effect, bad feng shui, the revenge effect—that require precautionary measures. In Asia and increasingly throughout the world, feng shui determines and assesses such risks and provides remedies. Its methods for instilling high trust in the forecasting horizon have been relied on for millennia to produce results.

Drawing conventions

Forget about the Greeks for a minute because China currently holds the record for the world's oldest map. *Zhao yutu* or 'map of the area of the mausoleum' shows the locations of buildings in the funerary architecture of Wang Cuo (reigned 344 to 313 BCE) and his consorts. The map indicates more than 70 locations and is scaled at 1 : 500. But most importantly for our purposes is that south is positioned at the top of the map. You will find this convention used in feng shui when the mountain (sitting direction) is drawn at the bottom ('north') and the water (facing direction) is drawn facing up ('south') (see Figures 3.1 and 3.3).

Astronomical issues

Cosmic systems convey a speculative attempt to understand the world based on small solar effects in the environment. Ancient Chinese culture provides thousands of years of written materials on the study of cosmic effects. What is most intriguing is how much these extremely old studies complement scientific research.

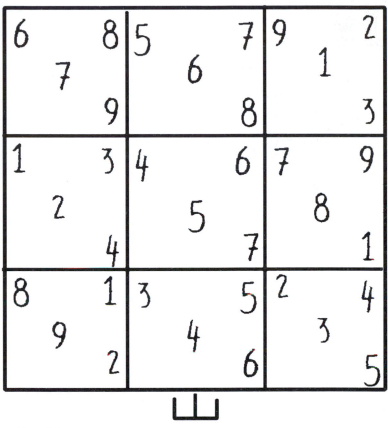

Figure 3.3

A rudimentary feng shui analysis with the sitting direction at the bottom and the facing direction at the top. The Chinese character *shan*, 'mountain', identifies the sitting direction.

Space weather, geomagnetism, and feng shui

Daoism aims to conform to the laws of nature. Ancient 'natural scientists' and later Daoists observed, recorded, and contemplated natural phenomena and cycles to better understand natural laws and to provide people with guidelines for living. Daoist emphasis on an understanding of human place in nature generated technology

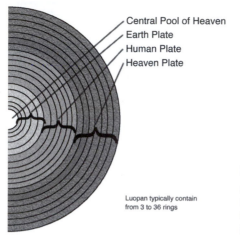

Central Pool of Heaven
Earth Plate
Human Plate
Heaven Plate

Luopan typically contain
from 3 to 36 rings

Figure 3.4

A diagram of one type of Luopan
(the three basic types used today
consist of San He, San Yuan,
and Zong He).

and natural science. They seem to have been very busy people, because they also discovered sunspots and geomagnetism. However, contrary to New Age belief, geomagnetism was not realized from psychic ability or intuition—magnetite in the human brain is not found in the same form as that observed in creatures relying on magnetoreception.[3]

More than 50 years ago, Professor Max Knoll provided intriguing research that feng shui tracks space weather in the form of ion radiation and contrary cyclical effects, including climatic changes and induced Earth currents. Whether or not the research is convincing, most scientists agree that feng shui practitioners observe geomagnetic field anomalies (low-amplitude, localized magnetic irregularities in space-time) with their Luopans (see Figure 3.4).

Never try to fool Mother Nature

Feng shui siting and calculations require knowledge of the precise orientation of a site or structure to create an event model. One or more readings with a Luopan are taken to determine orientation to the local magnetic field.

Besides measuring direction, magnetic declination, and the horizontal and vertical intensity of magnetic fields (called *dip*), a

Luopan provides qualitative observation of magnetic storms—especially whenever there are high magnetic field gradients. Depending on what technicians are seeking determines when they want to take their readings—amidst a howling geomagnetic storm or when the geomagnetic field is quiet.

Some ill-advised individuals think the Luopan's use is confined to finding the north magnetic pole. However, one would not need such a complex instrument, or need to apply the many complex formulae used in traditional feng shui, to accomplish this task. Besides, if we are looking for the magnetic pole we are actually looking for its *average position*, because it wanders daily in a rough ellipsis and may frequently move as much as 80 km off the mark when the Earth's magnetic field is disturbed. (Space weather in 1989 caused instruments that steer the heads of drilling equipment in North Sea oil exploration to register compass readings that varied by as much as 12°.) This happens because the daylight side of our planet faces the solar particle stream and then, as night approaches, the dark side faces away from the stream. Because of this effect early morning or late afternoon generally remain the best times for baseline Luopan readings.

The magnetic field measured by a Luopan, the *main field* of Earth, actually consists of several magnetic fields produced by a variety of overlapping sources, and it extends tens of thousands of kilometers into space. More than 90 per cent of the geomagnetic field is generated by the Earth's outer core. Other fields include magnetized elements of the Earth's crust, electric currents in the ionosphere and magnetosphere (the magnetic field generated by currents flowing in the ionized layers of the Earth's atmosphere occurs when streams of particles or *proton events* arrive from the sun), and the effects of ocean currents. Other possible influences on a Luopan if a practitioner is not careful include the magnetism of manufactured objects such as railroads, metal buildings, cars, and fences. All geomagnetic fields vary in space and in time periods that range from fractions of a second (micropulsations) to millions of years (magnetic reversals).[4]

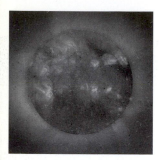

Figure 3.5

The sun displayed at the wavelength of iron—Fe XV (284 Å). Taken in the evening of 28 February 2000, by SOHO's Extreme-Ultraviolet Imaging Telescope. Courtesy of the EIT Consortium and National Oceanic and Atmospheric Administration, Space Environment Center (http://www.sec.noaa.gov/).

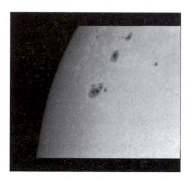

Figure 3.6

Sunspots captured in a large-scale White Light image of Region 8594. Received 99/06/22 at 14:31 Holloman AFB, New Mexico. National Oceanic and Atmospheric Administration, Space Environment Center (http://www.sec.noaa.gov/).

Every 27 days the sun blasts a particle stream our way. Earth's magnetic field undergoes a daily high (daylight) and low (darkness) period, a 27-day period of low- and medium-level storms, and a 30-day period of intense storms. Sunspots exhibit a cycle of 33.33 years with a maxima every 100 years. Double peaks of solar maxima are separated by 18 months. There is a 155-day cycle of solar flares and a 16-month rhythm at the base of the sun's convection zone. The sun's magnetic field reverses approximately every 11 years, around the peak of the sunspot cycle. The 11-year cycle may be related to the orbit of *Sui*, Jupiter. The solar magnetic field evolves over the solar cycle along with the sunspot number, which means there is an approximately 22-year cycle in the sun's magnetic polarity (see Figures 3.5 and 3.6).

Geomagnetic and ionospheric storm maxima occur at the equinoxes in generally double the amount of storms encountered

Figure 3.7

Aurora borealis display near Anchorage, Alaska, in 1977. Treasures of the NOAA Library Collection—Historic NWS Collection. Photographer: Doctor Yohsuke Kamide, Nagoya University. From the collection of Dr Herbert Kroehl, NGDC.

Figure 3.8

Aurora australis at Antarctica, South Pole Station, in 1979. Treasures of the NOAA Library Collection—NOAA Corps Collection. Photographer: Commander John Bortniak, NOAA Corps.

during summer and winter. (Interestingly, the first 'seasons' recognized by many ancient cultures—including the Chinese—were marked by the equinoxes, not the solstices.) In geomagnetic storms, electric currents travel along the planet's latitudinal fields and create an inaudible 'wind' that moves from the auroral region to the lower latitudes (see Figures 3.7 and 3.8).

If particles hit Earth's surface they can confuse compasses and produce nearly direct currents in transmission lines that knock

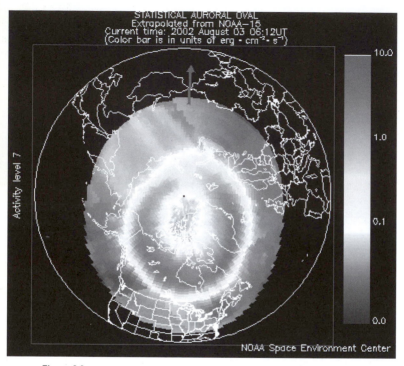

Figure 3.9

Data from NOAA POES satellite. Centre time of most recent polar pass measurement: 3 August 2002 0438 UT. National Oceanic and Atmospheric Administration, Space Environment Center (http://www.sec.noaa.gov/).

out power systems, create malfunctions in machinery, and cause massive blackouts. In August 1972, a transformer at the British Columbia Hydroelectric Authority exploded when shifting magnetic fields generated a current spike. In March 1989, space weather hit the power grid in North America and left large parts of Canada, Sweden, and the United States sitting in the dark (see Figure 3.9).

Long, uninterrupted stretches of pipe can also convey solar storms to the surface, and the storm currents affect pipelines by amplifying corrosion. Space weather in June 1989 created enough corrosive effects on a gas pipeline that it exploded and took with it part of the Trans-Siberian Railway, two passenger trains, and 500 people.

You do not really need to know all this to perform a feng shui analysis, but it helps to understand exactly what is being measured and how science and feng shui agree.

The flaming ring of fire

One ring on a Luopan consists of 24 seasons and climates: the 12 *jieqi* (minor solar terms that include equinoxes and solstices) and 12 *zhongqi* (major solar terms). The markings indicate the solar cycle determined by the tropical year, and they show good agreement with the annual frequency of magnetic storms. A total of 360 *du* (degrees) contain 24 four-week periods of 15 days. Every 15° the sun passes on the ecliptic indicates one of these solar energy nodes. Every 30° ticks off a month (interestingly, there is a 30-year cycle of Saturn through the ecliptic but Chinese set it to 28 years). This means that the Loupan ring functions like a clock—in fact, you can use this ring to measure time as an angle. On a San Yuan Luopan you can combine constellations with the 24 Mountains to track time.

In China, the seasons and climates measured on a Luopan still match the growing cycle and function as a farmer's calendar with a year that begins at midnight at the winter solstice (Zi)—just as the official calendar did during the Zhou period (see Table 3.1). Notice that the four beginnings mark quarter-days that were commonly used throughout the Neolithic world in farmers' calendars and astronomy in monuments (such as Newgrange).

The *Yi Jing* pairs the 24 nodes in Table 3.1 to create 12 months in fluctuating combinations of yin and yang. The months are more than just 'moonths', for the 'year' of Jupiter also begins at the winter solstice, heralded by the year-marker *Xing Ji* (during the Han period this was the star Spica, in our constellation of the Virgin). Now the solar terms provide four seasons, 12 months, and 72 weeks.

Table 3.1

The 24 climatic periods of the solar cycle with Gregorian dates and solar longitude

Period	Approximate Gregorian date	Solar longitude
Beginning of Spring	5 February	315
Rain	20 February	330
Excited Insects	7 March	345
Spring Equinox	22 March	0
Clear and Bright	6 April	15
Grain Rain	21 April	30
Beginning of Summer	6 May	45
Lesser Fullness	22 May	60
Ripening Grain	7 June	75
Summer Solstice	22 June	90
Slight Heat	8 July	105
Great Heat	24 July	120
Beginning of Autumn	8 August	135
End of Heat	24 August	150
White Dew	8 September	165
Autumn Equinox	24 September	180
Cold Dew	9 October	195
Descent of Frost	24 October	210
Beginning of Winter	8 November	225
Lesser Snow	23 November	240
Great Snow	7 December	255
Winter Solstice	22 December	270
Slight Cold	6 January	285
Great Cold	21 January	300

Interestingly, two feng shui techniques pair the solar periods with the 24 Mountains and calculate clockwise (*Daiyang*, the orbit of Jupiter) or anticlockwise (*Daiyin*, the invisible, counterorbital version of Jupiter). Whatever is to the left or 'ahead' of Daiyin is diminished; whatever is to the right or 'behind' Daiyin is increased. Daiyang and Daiyin provide additional date calculations, and of course the 24 Mountains form the backbone of orientation calculations.

This information gets factored into calculations because you want a structure to sync with the position of the sun and save on energy costs, just as you want it to harmonize with local manifestations of space weather and the local magnetic field.

Bad feng shui? A scientific opinion

The orientation of Earth's magnetic axis relative to the sun modifies the magnetosphere's response to the solar wind. Changing air pressure fronts produce fluctuations in the active oxygen content of the atmosphere through air currents coming from the stratosphere or out of cavities in the soil. Winds blowing down from the stratosphere create fluctuations of ozone concentration at sea level.[5] The resulting excess or deficiency of active oxygen disturbs the balance of the autonomous nervous system. Asthma sufferers and those with respiratory allergies and chemical sensitivities can experience adverse symptoms at lower concentrations of ozone.[6]

Frequencies of brainwaves in humans span the range of electromagnetic micropulsations and the oscillations of geomagnetic storms, but geomagnetic storms are considerably more intense than our brainwaves. That is why there are links between mental illness and geomagnetic field conditions, and geomagnetic activity corresponds with convulsions and heart attacks.[7] A few studies indicate a correspondence of death rate, disease rate, auroral activity, magnetic storms, and the 27-day rotation of the sun. Deaths may be related to climatic phenomena caused by ion concentration. Anecdotal evidence indicates that people suffering from chronic illness feel their ailment more acutely at the solstices and equinoxes thanks to the effects of space weather. Other 'meteorologically challenged' individuals include people suffering from stress, people who are generally sensitive to weather fluctuations, and individuals exhibiting certain kinds of mental illness. Problems can manifest not unlike orientation problems suffered by birds during an atmospheric disturbance.

Figure

Lightning storm over Boston circa 1967. Treasures o
NOAA Library Collection—Historic NWS Collec
Photographer: *Boston G.*

It is shocking

Human bodies can serve as partial electrical conductors and low-frequency fields induce electric currents in humans, hence the potential for biological harm. However, this does not explain the New Age obsession with the natural extra low frequency resonance better known as *Schumann Resonance* (SR). Some believe SR is a planetary-mind field because SR cycles in the range of human brainwaves—1.5–4 Hz (delta waves), 5–8 Hz (theta waves), 9–14 Hz (alpha waves), or 15–40 Hz (beta waves). Of course the truth is not quite as exciting (see Figure 3.10).

Schumann Resonance is a frequency from 5 to 50 Hz that can create a resonating cavity when activated in the gap between the Earth and the ionosphere. Substantial variations in the strength of the field occur according to global deviations in lightning activity detected by sensitive equipment. Lightning activity around the globe is particularly responsive to changes in planetary temperature. This explains why SR is substantially stronger in June than in January. However, worldwide measuring stations record the strongest signals in April, when the tropics are at their hottest. The semiannual seasonal effect is measured in the intensity of the vertical electric field and horizontal magnetic field. Peak frequencies can vary daily by ± 0.5 Hz from their smallest average values. Frequency variation also depends on whether a measurement is made from north to south or east to west.

I mention this only because one corollary activity of some feng shui adepts was the study of winds (*fengjiao*). Wind seasons (*fengzhi*) tracked the orbit of Mercury and used its movements in computations for cold and famine. There were eight winds to a 360-day year divided into periods according to *ganzhi* (the 60-year cycle). The device they used during the periods of Warring States, Qin, and early Han—a peculiar astrolabe known as a *shi*—was used to track Beidou and correlate the wind seasons. Practitioners kept oral (and eventually written) records of lightning 'seasons'. From celestial and meteorological observations, a military leader or attaché could read the outcome of a battle by *tianshu* (celestial

mathematics). In Chinese science, the interaction of yin and yang in the atmosphere produces thunder and lightning and links to the process of evaporation from bodies of water. Using this system, ancient feng shui practitioners donated their services to the community as the local weather forecasters.

Look up in the sky!

The *Book of Odes* claims the *kanyu shia* of the Zhou used a compass to read the landscape. *Kanyu* is the traditional time-calculation aspect of feng shui. A *kanyu shia* was an expert in this method and a *feng shui xiansheng* was a feng shui expert who could be an expert in *kanyu* and a variety of other calculation techniques, which is why many adepts in the Han period were called *fang shi*, 'experts

in methods'. Based on the archeology of feng shui devices and on literary references, the shi astrolabe was not a magnetic compass. A *shi* contains markings a present-day feng shui practitioner would recognize, but techniques differed somewhat. For one, it relied more on astronomy.

As described in ancient texts, in Neolithic China the Hetu served as a climate indicator for eastern China, and the Luoshu provided an astral compass so that traders going to Western Asia and farther afield could find their way home. Longshan black pottery came from what is now Iran; some of Lady Hao's ancient jade pieces came from just as far to the west of Shang territories.

According to one analysis, the centre of the Hetu is a quincunx that indicates the circumpolar region. Above and below the quincunx are black dots indicating the square shape of Earth. From the Mawangdui manuscripts we know the Hetu was used by forecasters in the Warring States and Qin periods to calculate movements of Daiyin beginning each year around 4 February in the Gregorian calendar. In contemporary feng shui the Hetu is used to analyse water features.

Before the shi was invented, an astronomer observed the celestial objects that crossed the north–south meridian in their daily motion. This information could be coded into any number of systems— myths, diagrams, and buildings. The symbols and ancient usage of Hetu and Luoshu were absorbed into the *shi*, also called a *liuren* astrolabe, which gradually evolved into a contemporary Luopan. In fact, a *shi* is like the Hetu, with its four 'rings' of black and white dots. The five dots at the centre of the Hetu were eventually replaced by the Celestial Lake or Central Pool of Heaven on a compass (the needle housing).

The next ring of numbers conforms to the Inside Plate or Heaven Plate (the round plate which on older devices shows Beidou or provides the base for the ladle). Out from that ring of dots is the square Earth Plate in which the Heaven Plate sits. On *shi* and the later *shipan* it contains the markings. The quincunx also identifies the

A Qin period shi (liuren astrolabe) showing the back (left) and front (right) sides

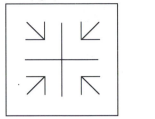 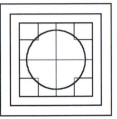

A Han period Shipan (Sometimes called a Sinan), the oldest working magnetic compass (left) and the hierogamy of the baguas that echoes the earlier designs (right)

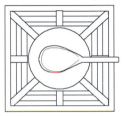

SE		S		SW
	Dui	Qian	Xun	
	4	9	2	
E	Li 3	5	7 Kan	W
	8	1	6	
	Zhen	Kun	Gen	
NE		N		NW

Figure 3.11

Before the Luopan existed the *sinan*; before the *sinan* there was the *shi* (*shipan* or *liuren* astrolabe).

Heaven Centre Cross Line or Red Cross Grid, the warp and woof of heaven—considered the axle of the universe or *ya-xing* because it is north–south (*zi–wu*) and east–west (*mao-yu*). These red strings or cross markings are used to read direction and meaning, but also indicate equinoctial and solstitial colures. They are part of the Earth Plate on a *shi* and *shipan* (see Figure 3.11).

We know feng shui is old and that it works in fair agreement with scientific understanding of space weather. But what can it do for us?

Notes

[1] Geomancy (literally *earth-prophecy*) consists of divination by dot patterns formed according to precise rules about random figures drawn in the dirt. Each pattern has a name (such as Amissio, Fortuna Major, Puella, and Rubeus). The two 'constellations' Puella and Rubeus

are found in a discussion of *geomancie* in Geoffrey Chaucer's *Canterbury Tales*. You can find a few mentions of geomancy in Shakespeare's plays.

[2] Traditional knowledge constitutes a cumulative body of knowledge, know-how, practices, and representations maintained and developed by people with extended histories of interaction with the natural world. It originated independently of science in a particular cultural setting, and typically independent of Western culture. Traditional knowledge is not intended to compete with science, but it is well established in scientific circles as strengthening traditional science and contributing to a wide variety of sustainable development practices that range from medicine to environmental management. The challenge faced by scientists is to define traditional knowledge in a way that recognizes its value and does justice to its traditions without giving credibility to pseudoscience (International Council for Science, 2002b).

[3] See Mielczarek and McGrayne (2000). Magnetite levels in human brains increase with the severity of Alzheimer's and other neurodegenerative diseases such as Huntington's and Parkinson's.

[4] Researchers recently discovered a reversed magnetic field in two regions of the boundary between the Earth's core and its overlying mantle. Beneath the southern tip of Africa the magnetic field points toward the centre of the Earth, a phenomenon that runs counter to the dominant outward-pointing field in the Southern Hemisphere.

[5] In temperate latitudes, winter is when air from the Earth's stratosphere drops to ground level. The typical level of ozone in the atmosphere at sea level is approximately 0.05 parts per million. Research indicates that below temperatures of 22–26 °C (70–80 °F) no relationship exists between ozone concentrations and temperature. Above 32 °C (90 °F), a strong and positive relationship exists.

[6] Ozone decays to normal oxygen in approximately 30 min after it forms, but during this time it reacts with nearby molecules to form various oxides. At concentrations below approximately 1 part per million ozone exhibits a pleasant and characteristic odour typically described as the smell in the air following a thunderstorm. Concentrations higher than 2 parts per million convey a pungent odour reminiscent of chlorine. Concentrations little greater than 1 part per million create headaches; decreased pulse rate and blood pressure; tears; dermatitis; and eye, nose, and respiratory irritations. Increasing concentrations intensify the severity of symptoms and ultimately cause pulmonary oedema and chronic respiratory disease.

[7] Campbell (1997, pp. 242–3).

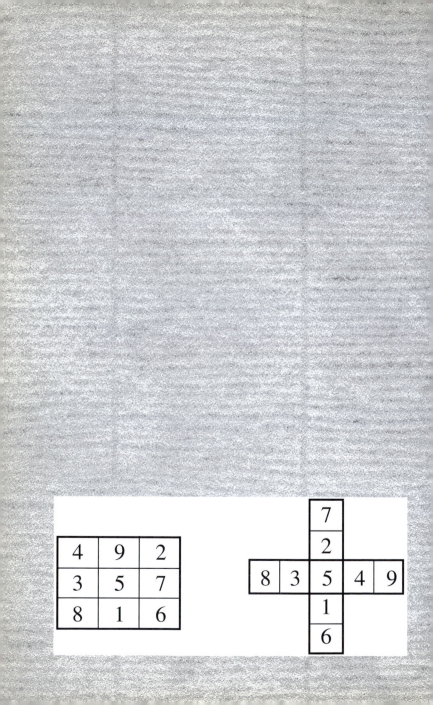

Chapter 4

Calculations

*Y*ou must be feeling a bit overwhelmed by now if you previously assumed feng shui is all about finding a Relationship Corner or a Money Corner, or depends on the first thing we see upon entering a building.

A basic theory of McFengshui is that we are drawn inexorably to whatever our eyes alight on first, which, in turn, affects how we proceed on entering. These 'first impressions' supposedly provide suggestions for someone to elaborate on the significance of the encounter. The problem with this kind of thinking is that the image at the eye has countless possible interpretations. Humans construct what they see and as a minimum they also construct what they hear, smell, taste, and feel—all human perceptions and sensations are constructions. This is why we can construct feelings in parts of our bodies that have been surgically removed.[1] In addition, humans are often quite unaware of environmental details from one moment to the next. We perceive and remember only whatever we concentrate on and can fail to notice a gorilla standing right in front of us.[2]

The theory of 'brain plasticity' suggests that all human sense organs function like input devices, and our brains can adapt to new data channels simply by creating new synapses. That is why fighter pilots wear suits that provide physical feedback (to lessen the reliance on instrumentation), and will soon be navigating solely by images buzzing their tongues. The same technique has been used to provide visual information to the blind, who can in turn 'see' whatever is presented in this fashion.[3] It is hard to take the 'first impressions' idea seriously when people can experience entering your home by 'seeing' it on their tongues.

Numerical conventions

Luoshu, Hetu, and valuations

Rest assured, this chapter is not meant to be a 'how-to' on theories and techniques, or a substitute for study with a good teacher. (Refer to Chapter 15 for schools and educational materials.) The

information in this chapter merely provides one way of looking at this material.

Feng-shui experts employ a variety of numerical attributes and equivalents with formulae for particular techniques. These lists originate in feng-shui texts, many of them more than 2000 years old, and with traditional teachers who have passed their formulae and techniques to their students. The material keeps adapting to new structures, new materials, and new settlements—but always within guidelines.

As mentioned in Chapter 2 (*Time and Space*), each season and each element is assigned a numeric value. This value is part of the analogy map shown in Table 4.1. The list by no means exhausts the attributes for each number; more can be found in the arrangements of the diagrams used for calculations. The manifest strength of an attribute depends on whether the attribute is inherently yin or yang and whether it is expressed in the native or *wang* cycle of the building. During the 180-year life cycle (see Chapter 10), the internal balance of yin and yang in each number shifts so that eventually even the best (most yang) valuation is heavily flavoured with yin.

Doing your own calculations

Providing feng-shui analyses is not a task for the novice because so much is at stake—especially in revenge effects. According to the ethics provided by the top feng-shui instructors (based on Daoist codes of ethics), revenge effects created by practitioners return to disturb practitioners. Simple carelessness—such as taking an inappropriate stance to use a Luopan—can distort the reading. Egregious errors, furthermore, run you the risk of litigation (bringing court cases against feng-shui practitioners is quite common in Asia—some practitioners are sentenced to gaol). Much is at stake and a practitioner should be capable of the challenge. For all of these reasons and more, teachers use their current projects as case studies for their students so that they can reap the benefits of on-site education—and not practice on paying clients.

Table 4.1

Baseline qualities during a structural life cycle of 180 years

Number	Positive expression	Negative expression
1	Abundance, distinction, intelligence	Divorce, disconnection, ignorance
2	Well-being, wholeness	Disabilities and ailments
3	Fluency, persuasiveness	Conflict, prosecution
4	Enthusiasm, erudition	Infidelity and scandal
5	Prosperity and accomplishment	Disaster and misfortune
6	Authority and leadership	Vanity, insensitivity, aloofness
7	Spirituality, metaphysics	Grievances and larceny
8	Monetary abundance	Tremors, seizures
9	Advancement, matriculation	Auditory and visual problems, fires

Pros and cons

The genuine depth and sophistication of traditional feng shui intimidates many people—especially anyone used to the sound-bite psychobabble of the McFengshui.[4] Do not assume you can pop into a bookseller and walk out with a complete how-to book, because even the *best* feng-shui books admit they are not comprehensive! That is why you can find basic books on the Xuan Kong subdiscipline Flying Stars, not on all of Xuan Kong. Unfortunately, the majority of books on feng shui were written by hacks for interior designers, not people designing buildings or developing property. Moreover, they typically discuss little more than lifestyle issues of the developed world.

Working with a practitioner

Finding a competent practitioner requires an interview process. Know what you need for the job and be prepared to interview until

you find someone to do the job you need and work within your plan. Exercise due diligence to avoid your own revenge effects.

A word about marketing

Feng-shui marketing often gives the impression that a practitioner's services provide wide-ranging environmental benefits—including the ability to relieve a variety of spurious problems such as the popular but nonexistent 'geopathic stress'. The US Federal Trade Commission (FTC) considers it deceptive to misrepresent in any way that a service offers a *general* environmental benefit (ISO 14000 was developed primarily from the FTC's guidelines). Moreover, environmental marketing claims should not exaggerate or overstate attributes or benefits. Specific environmental claims are easier to substantiate than general claims and less likely to be deceptive.

Unfortunately, most feng-shui books and websites seem to have lifted their marketing from *Scams from the Great Beyond* (Huston, 1997), and appear intent on adding another chapter to *Extraordinary Popular Delusions and the Madness of Crowds* (Mackay, 1841). The scientifically valid claims that relate to feng shui primarily rely on evidence regarding the effects of the natural environment on human physiology, behaviour, and psychology (see Chapter 7).

An unqualified, general claim of environmental benefit may communicate that a service provides extensive environmental benefits when it in fact it does not—unfortunately, this is all too often the case with feng-shui marketing. Anyone making express or implied claims about the attributes of their product, package, or service *must* have a reasonable basis for their assertions. A 'reasonable basis' might require competent and reliable evidence (tests, analyses, research, studies, or other evidence based on the expertise of peers). Sadly, you will generally find that the McFengshui crowd bristles at the mere mention of this amount of scrutiny, while plenty of traditional practitioners would jump at the chance to document what feng shui can do.

Above all, do not fall prey to popular marketing scams that rely on anecdotal evidence such as the popular 'testimonials'.

Finding competent help

Interview prospective practitioners. Do they use a Luopan, and which one do they prefer? Can they name and perform any of the calculations? (Some people tell prospective clients that they practice 'form school' but cannot name or perform calculations, or name the compass used for calculations.) Have they had extensive study and experiment under the watchful eye of instructors? (You do not want someone practicing on *you*—especially with your financial support.) How many hours of education and what levels have been attained? Have you ever heard of the teacher or school? Does the school curriculum agree with what is taught by the majority of the top Asian masters?

Do terms like 'geopathic stress' and other nonexistent nonsense creep into their conversation?

Another 'new age' money machine, geopathic stress has no basis in legitimate science.[5] Proponents claim it originates in geomagnetic radiation distorted by electromagnetism emitted by the water table, particular mineral deposits (a list of minerals that constantly varies), earthquake fault lines, and underground caverns or cavities.[6] The distortions create problems for anything living on the surface (but apparently not *under*). Naturally, a variety of modern contrivances conveniently cause the same problems—at unspecified frequencies. The most common 'geopathic' complaints result from fuse boxes, power lines,[7] and a variety of towers. Apparently, people find the geopathic culprits by dowsing (a form of spontaneous divination).

A German physician claims to have discovered a terrestrial grid (the Earth's 'aura' according to some proponents) that dovetails neatly into these fanciful ideas. Supposedly the north–south lines of the 'Hartmann grid' are spaced at roughly 2.3 m and the east–west lines are spaced about every 2.5 m. People claim that the power of this grid emanates from the surface of Earth to heights that conveniently range from 20 m to nearly 10 km, while the supposed 'zone' of these lines can influence organisms at distances from under 1 to 60 m.[8] The physician claimed that harmful radiation emanates more powerfully at the intersections of the gridlines, although this radiation is concomitantly believed to emanate in all directions. A variety of lucrative careers such as baubiology and pseudo-geobiology[9] service this nonexistent 'problem' and claim feng shui as the historical antecedent.

Is the term 'energy' used indiscriminately when *willpower* or *personal exertion* is really being meant?

Energy is generally defined by science as the capacity to do work. Energy cannot be created from nothing, it must be obtained from somewhere else.

Does everything 'mean' something, from the positioning of the cat's litterbox to the condition of a piece of furniture?

Is there an obsession with clutter?

Does the individual practise spontaneous divination (the so-called 'intuitive' feng-shui) to gather knowledge about a structure, or is the assessment based on an accumulation of facts?

Renovations

Many times a client hires a feng-shui consultant and an architect to help with a remodel project. Often the feng-shui consultant is hired to ensure that the construction proceeds smoothly and the desired effect is obtained. Sometimes they make suggestions regarding design particulars (the flow of rooms, where services are installed, etc.). Although it may seem a practitioner is trying to tell you how to do your job, they really want to help you excel at your job and provide your client with the best possible results. If a feng-shui practitioner can help you to avoid construction revenge effects that

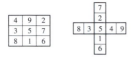

prevent the client from paying their bills (including your fee), would you let them?

Pros and cons

For many people feng shui is a terrific 'new age' swindle. The novel *Fixer Chao* (Ong, 2001) contains the character of a feng-shui faker inspired by McFengshui versions of feng-shui. A good practitioner can provide a wealth of information if you provide only a compass reading, a construction and/or move-in date, and a birth date. It is not rocket science, but it is not gilded with symbolism and meaningless references to 'energy' either.

Notes

[1] See Hoffman et al. (2000).

[2] See Simons and Chabris (1999).

[3] See Bach-y-Rita et al. (1998) and University Communications (2001).

[4] A typically glowing assessment is that feng shui provides 'keys for creating the future you desire', as if it was a personal organiser (DeAmicis and DeAmicis, 2001).

[5] Geopathic stress has escaped detection by flux-gate sensors, optically pumped or alkali-vapour sensors, gradiometers, magnetic microgravity surveys, proton magnetometers, rubidium optically pumped magnetometers, cryogenic magnetometers, soil conductivity meters, and superconducting, quantum interference device (SQUID) magnetometers. You will not find geopathic stress mentioned in any scientific journals, although there is plenty on how spectral magnetic disturbances depend on the amount of geomagnetic activity, and how the dynamics of Earth's magnetosphere depend on the orientation of the interplanetary magnetic field (Cowley et al., 2002; Rees et al., 2002).

[6] Strangely, proponents of this odd idea do not mention outgassing of the mantle as an issue, and assume that what we stand on is solid—rather than a series of concentric spheres, with the top layer (primarily composed of silicates) only 38-km thick (Ballentine et al., 2002; Grossman, 2002).

[7] US power lines operate in the range of 70–765 kV and minimize the electric field.

[8] Contrast this information with scientific study of the troposphere, where life is found and weather occurs. It averages 11 km above Earth but 8 km above the poles and 16 km above the equator (Suzuki and McConnell, 1998, p. 41).

[9] *Geobiology* in legitimate science is generally defined as 'the present and past interactions between life and inanimate matter' (American Academy of Microbiology, 2000). 'Geobiology' as pseudoscience has the goal of enabling people to reproduce a habitat 'as near to natural living conditions as possible' (Gobet, 1998). Proponents also tend to blather on about the 'technical, harmonic, and symbolic' levels realized in the built environment.

Chapter 5

Planning

*E*nvironmental planning attempts through informed decisions to integrate environmental and biophysical information into humanity's use of our planet. All well and good, but it has a poor record of mitigating revenge effects, and many of its 'informed decisions' have been based on greed and graft. Additionally, in urban planning the 'biophysical inventory'—a euphemism for *biota* or the nonhuman world—has no say in its use.

Any paradigm—and that includes environmental planning—sees only what it wants to see. One person's 'visual resource management' is another's *turfing*, defined by journalist Grady Clay as ingredients in the 'geometry of territoriality'. The demarcation of civic and private territories is often characterized by fuzzy, green triangular mounds ('pubic-hair greenery'), clipped hedges, sparse trees, and other low-maintenance ground cover—the lowest common denominator form of urban planning[1] (see Figure 5.1).

In the developed world, urban planning builds for automobiles, not for people. That is why a third of the land surface of Los Angeles is covered by freeways, other streets, and parking lots. If we are not to leave a diminished world to future generations we have to develop better ways of dealing with the natural world (see Figure 5.2).

Tradition—or not

In China, as in so many other cultures, the traditional house plan takes the form of a square or rectangle. Larger structures consist of connected squares, L-shapes, circles, or rectangles with courtyards in the middle. The Earth itself provides a primary source of shelter. More than 10 million Chinese still live in *yaodong*, houses dug out of the ground with only a courtyard showing from the surface. Traditional housing is not necessarily sustainable, but it provides ecological efficiency for a particular climate and topography. Revenge effects regularly occur only when people ignore local weather and landscape for arbitrary design considerations, illusion, and/or monetary benefits.

(a)

(b)

Figure 5.1(a, b)

Pubic-hair greenery at its finest. Photos by the author.

Figure 5.2

Salt Lake City, Utah. Image courtesy NASA/GSFC/MITI/ERSDAC/ JAROS, and U.S./Japan ASTER Science Team Satellite: Terra Sensor: ASTER Image Date: 05-28-2000.

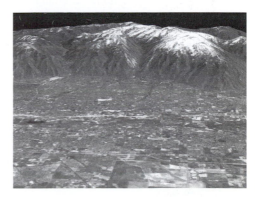

What you do not see in most traditional and sustainable buildings even at its most grandiose is the McMansion, which boffins deride as 'the fast-food version of the American dream'. A McMansion is a large suburban home seemingly built in cookie-cutter fashion. These structures are everywhere, like McDonald's restaurants.[2] (Sadly, in the 'develop and be damned' atmosphere of modern China, there is now an entire subdivision of McMansions north of Beijing.[3]) McMansions, like McRanches, McBungalows, and McMediterraneans provide generic, mass-produced housing. The structure is apparently designed to look like it has endured several generations of add-ons—although these houses commonly consist of pre-existing plans from developers that merely *advertise* architects on staff. (Clients are likely to meet only the workers and the project manager.) At the front of these McMansions—to emphasize what is really important—sits a 'garage Mahal', an extra wide and high garage that accommodates multiple cars and SUVs (see Figure 5.3).

pical McMansion and garage Mahal.

Crowding McMansions together exaggerates the effect of lots that appear small in proportion to the size of the houses, despite their adherence to local zoning and setback requirements. Sparse landscaping makes them look even more outlandish. The yards look bare because of 'clear-cutting': a developer hires a bulldozer for a few days and razes the site. At the end of the project the developer typically rolls out a s sod lawn, installs a few basic shrubs and very young trees, a few basic shrubs, and very young trees, then leaves the remainder of the landscaping to the buyers—who do not have the money for such trivialities because they are in debt to their eyeballs trying to afford their dream home.

McMansion subdivisions are usually saddled with names developed by a marketing department to sell a fantasy lifestyle. Posh universities, pseudo-British toponyms, and whatever vegetation and wildlife existed before the subdivision seem to be universally popular. However, many people buy into this fantasy lifestyle only to have it turn into a nightmare. Nearly all of these McHouses are site-blind and poorly built—the perfect complement to a barren spiritual landscape. Their revenge effects equal the destruction created during their development from clear-cutting, along with their negligent planning and workmanship.

In *How Buildings Learn*, Brand (1994) mentions that in the 1980s malpractice lawsuits against architects overtook lawsuits against doctors. Homeowners' malpractice lawsuits provide a litany of identical problems with McHouses beyond mere misrepresentation—framing errors, insufficient foundation structures, fireplaces that are in multiple violation of state building codes, improper attic ventilation due to roofing deficiencies, deviation from (pre-existing) architect's plans, siding problems, insulation problems leading to increased humidity and growth of toxic moulds within the living spaces (*Stachybotrys chartarum, aspergillus*, and *penicillium*), water leaks, cracked foundations, shoddy stucco, cracked floors, doors that do not close properly, bathroom fixtures that do not work, and back yards that flood regularly. Some builders have had to buy back parts of neighbourhoods after complaints or lawsuits over problem homes.

In some cases, local government is as much to blame as poor workmanship. Many councils relax one or more building guidelines when they approve projects, especially critical ones like soil studies, which are used to determine the extent of grading for home foundations. Later come the malpractice lawsuits due to severe revenge effects, like homes sliding down the hill, or toxic mould.

And people wonder why they need feng shui!

Form and shape theory

Many feng-shui experts consider form and shape analysis to be the foremost study of environmental influences. Known as the Three Combination School or *San He*, this is widely accepted as the oldest school of feng shui still in regular use. While more ancient types exist, such as calculations of *Xing-De*, their use apparently died out and can be only partly revived by scholarship.

Without assessing form and shape no genuine understanding of a site's feng shui is possible. The objective is to gently place structures and entities in the natural flow of the land.

Analyses by a variety of researchers into favourable structural locations (*xue*)[4] according to traditional rules of feng shui demonstrate these locations comprise highly suitable microclimates. Ancient feng-shui experts said these locations provide the ability to accumulate creative potential. Such positioning also promotes the integration of human construction into the natural environment as it enhances carrying capacity.

An assessment of form and shape for a site consists of three components:

- *Physical environment*. This consists of land mass, open space, and water.
- *Topography*. This consists of specific effects on sites of the positions and flow of water and land.
- *Directional and vicinity influences*. This includes microclimate analysis and can encompass *Ba Zhai* (a calculation technique).

Form and shape theory combines yin and yang theory with certain elements of five-element theory, topography, calendar science, and astronomy. It correlates the 24 solar periods with cardinal and inter-cardinal directions. The practitioner analyses mountains by shape, position, and taxonomy. Any bodies of water are likewise noted and analysed. Compass readings determine additional characteristics, relationships, and potential. Practitioners identify the developed environment by the same rules. Buildings assume the characteristics of mountains and valleys. Roads are analysed according to the criteria for water.

Traditional analytical techniques consisted of looking, listening and smelling, asking, and feeling—deceptively simple terms that can be defined comprehensively or superficially depending on the practitioner. Today, we have the opportunity to add statistical analysis and other scientific tools to the ancient feng-shui analytical techniques and create a neotraditional approach.

Principles and terminology

Traditional sources define 'auspicious feng shui' as positions in space-time meeting the following criteria:

- *Good celestial influences*. This can be superficially interpreted as traditional cosmological influences, or interpreted more broadly as favourable bioclimatic as well as conventional influences.
- *Good geographical features*. In general, a site determined to have 'good features' provides favourable conditions, a site with 'disorganized features' supplies no positive features, while a site with 'malevolent features' provides adverse and even hostile conditions. 'Good form' for a building or a hill consists of strong, defined slopes and an undamaged shape that makes it easily categorized. 'Bad form' consists of unidentifiable or confusing shapes and deteriorating conditions.
- *Human population in harmony with the environment*. This is measured, in general, by the emphasis of natural over human effects and evidence of widespread social equity, along with

quality of life issues. 'Bad form' and 'bad feng shui' encompass ecosystem decay (including habitat fragmentation), energy efficiency, health, and issues of acoustics.

Sites are analysed according to the following conditions:

- *Power.* Expresses the qualitative features of a component of a site in terms of subjective but experiential perceptions of its effects. Rivers, canyons, valleys, and mountains provide powerful nodes and edges. Their immense sizes can be considered strengths. Street traffic (interpreted as water) can aid some homes and annoy others on the same block.
- *Form.* Communicates qualities of a particular component of the site determined by the shape of buildings, hills, roads, and water features.
- *Structure.* Conveys relationships between geographic and/or built features of an area.
- *Condition.* Expresses relationships between features near a site.

Buildings and hills

Natural and artificial forms are identified according to the five-element theory, or catalogued in accordance with a nonary system that manifests astronomy and time in the landscape.

Taxonomy of five-element theory

Identification of buildings according to five element theory consists of the following:

- *Wood.* Indicates a shape with nearly vertical slopes and a gently rounded peak (a shrub shape).
- *Fire.* Describes a shape with a steep ascent and a sharp peak (a flame shape).
- *Soil.* Specifies a shape with nearly vertical slopes and a flat peak (a mesa or plateau shape).[5]
- *Metal.* Distinguishes a shape with very gentle slopes and a rounded peak (a bell shape).

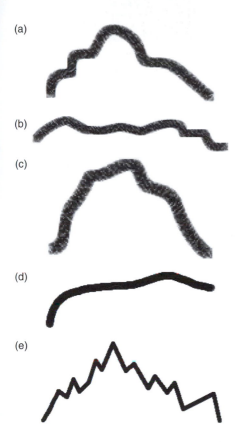

(a)

(b)

(c)

(d)

(e)

Figure 5.4

Identifying buildings and hills (from lowest elevation to highest): (a) a wood structure and hill; (b) a water structure and hill; (c) a soil structure and hill; (d) a metal structure and hill; (e) a fire structure and hill.

- *Water*. Identifies a shape with gentle, uneven slopes and one or more undulating peaks (a waveform) (see Figure 5.4).

Taxonomy of nine stars

Nine stars taxonomy (such as that used in ba zhai) consists of an ideological construction of the type of *qi* that changes over time. The diagram uses the primary stars of Beidou, formed of the following:

- *Greedy Wolf*. Associated with the colour white. Each of the nine 'stars' indicates a corresponding astronomical marker. For example, Greedy Wolf (*Tan Lang*) is the star Sirius.

- *Wide Door or Gate Guard*. Described as the soil element and associated with the colour black.
- *Prosperity or Rewards*. Associated with the colour of jade.
- *Scholar or Literary Art*. Associated with the colour green.
- *Virtue*. Associated with the colour yellow.
- *Military*. Described as the metal element and associated with the colour white.
- *Breaker of Armies*. Associated with the colour red.
- *Taiyang, Left Assistant*. Described as the metal element and associated with the colour white.
- *Daiyin, Right Assistant*. Associated with the colour purple.

Valleys and recessed structures

These conditions are analysed as the opposite of buildings and hills. Identifying valleys according to form and shape consists of the following:

- *Wood*. A shape with nearly vertical descent and a gently rounded base.
- *Fire*. A shape with steep descent and a sharp base.
- *Soil*. A shape with nearly vertical descent and a flat base.
- *Metal*. A shape with very gentle descent and a rounded base.
- *Water*. A shape with gentle, uneven descent and one or more undulating bases (see Figure 5.5).

Roads and water features

'Water dragons' most typically consist of aquatic landscape patterns, arrangements of aquatic plants, and areas where groundwater lies near the soil surface.[6] Although roads can exhibit some of the features of a water dragon, they generally do not display the conventional shape of a dragon (which is the primary form of identification). Moreover, fast-moving water (or highways), stagnant water (perpetual gridlock or heavy stop-and-go traffic), and precipitous waterfalls cannot be considered true 'dragons'.

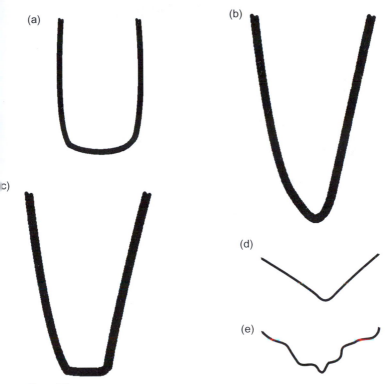

Figure 5.5

Identifying buildings and hills: (a) a wood structure and valley; (b) a fire structure and valley; (c) a soil structure and valley; (d) a metal structure and valley; (e) a water structure and valley.

From a scientific perspective, a meandering stream is a highly stable watercourse. A narrow, slow-moving street is ideal according to designers and promoters of the New Urbanism movement. Feng shui stresses comparable principles.

Determine the flow by the speed of traffic and whether traffic keeps to posted speed limits. Identify whether traffic-calming devices were installed, should be installed, or are being considered.

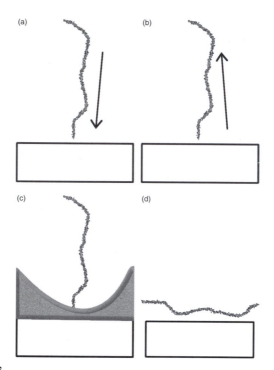

Figure 5.6

Identifying the flow of water and roads: (a) incoming water; (b) outgoing water; (c) gathering water; (d) horizontal water.

To analyse the flow of roads use the following rules that pertain to the flow of water:

- *Incoming water.* This identifies a road or water moving toward a site from the front (see Figure 5.6a).
- *Outgoing water.* This identifies a road or water moving away from a site (see Figure 5.6b).
- *Gathering water.* This identifies an area in front of a site where water or vehicles gather (including cars stopping to drop off shoppers, etc) (see Figure 5.6c).

- *Horizontal water*. This identifies a road moving in front of a site from one side to the other (see Figure 5.6d).
- *Absent and/or substitute water*. There is no road, or a road is needed and missing.

How water exits a site is as important as its entry to a site.

Development and redevelopment considerations

The primary purpose of feng shui is to build with the flow of the land. This means development maintains and follows the natural environment. Studies indicate that the use of this principle increases comfort, lowers costs, and reduces the need for artificial heating and/or cooling and irrigation. It diminishes or eliminates revenge effects.

Popular 'cut and fill' or 'clear-cutting' development produces an ugly, disharmonious landscape of bad feng shui notorious for its revenge effects. Proponents of this allegedly economical technique fail to consider the long-term consequences, including costs and maintenance. In the developing world, housing placed on deforested hillsides causes heavy flooding that destroys homes and lives. Typical structures in the developed world built on 'cut and fill' sites also possess inadequate protection against flooding. Drainage and similar problems are nearly impossible to solve and usually last the life of the structure. Moreover, typical designs provide little access by machinery to the back of a structure and require manual excavation work at a substantial increase in cost. Modifications can also involve substantial disruptions of the structure that further escalate suffering.

Feng shui stipulates that where the natural world has been destroyed it should be restored. Feng-shui principles express the need for harmony with local conditions and resources. This vision encourages the return of the so-called Disney Deserts[7] and other artificial settings to their natural state.[8] Restore habitat and wildlife to its proper place and provide evidence of human appreciation of the natural world. In cities this practice can lower the effect of heat islands that add to global change.

The following rules—many of which defy modern architectural and development techniques—are considered paramount in form and shape theory.

Buildings on a height should face flat or lower ground

Going with the flow of the land requires that a building situated on a hill should be supported by that hill much like someone sits on a chair and is supported by the chair's back. The ideal access is provided by an opening that moves from the lower ground in front to the higher ground (in effect against the flow). A building entered from the higher part to the lower part often imparts the sensation that it may tip backwards and tumble down the hill. My experience in a house of this type included the nearly overwhelming sensation that if I fell I would roll to the balcony and drop off. The house's position on the pad gave the impression it was built at a precarious slant (see Figure 5.7).

(a)

(b)

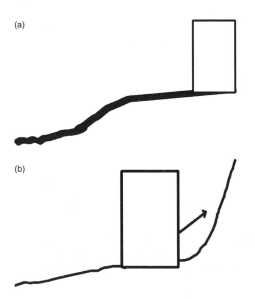

Figure 5.7

(a) Building on a height facing flat or lower ground. (b) Building on a height facing the wrong way.

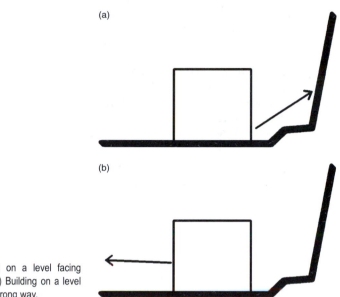

Figure 5.8

(a) Building on a level facing a height. (b) Building on a level facing the wrong way.

Buildings on a level should face a height

Structures on open, level terrain should face a taller building or a hill. This enables access to be arranged against the flow of the land while the structure sits with the flow (see Figure 5.8).

Face water whenever possible

'Waterfront property' conveys a particular meaning that is often thwarted by design. It is a cardinal rule of feng shui that the front of a structure situated near water should have its entry *facing* the water. (The biological reasons for this will be explored in a subsequent chapter.) A driveway should also terminate near the entrance facing the water. Entering from the opposite side of the water has a negative effect. Ideally, the mountain sits at the back and the water is at the front[9] (see Figure 5.9).

(a)

(b)

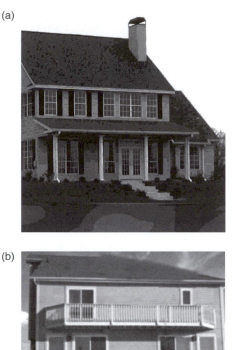

Figure 5.9

(a) A structure and entrance facing water. (b) A structure with an opposite entrance and the water behind.

Notes

[1] See Clay (1973, p. 153). The APA board of directors ratified the organization's principles of smart growth on 14 April 2002.

[2] McDonaldization has been defined as the process of integrating principles of fast-food restaurants into societies around the world (Ritzer, 1996).

[3] See Anton and Chu (2002).

[4] *Xue* roughly translates from Mandarin as a cave and/or a favourable residence location.

[5] The planning fashion of Walter Gropius provided for stark, minimalist, straight-sided buildings, especially as low-income projects. Now plagued by drugs, crime, and violence, these buildings are reviled as providing the least humane urban housing and neighbourhoods.

In feng shui, the number 5—soil—reflects these problems.

[6] A 'water dragon' in feng shui can consist of wetlands according to the Cowardin system used by the US government.

[7] According to the Phoenix, Arizona, District Forester/Fire Management Office, developers create a 'Disney Desert' when they defy native plant ordinances by slicking off native vegetation with backhoes at the beginning of construction, then replant with reclaimed on-site plant material supplemented with various nursery stock.

[8] Typical advice on this return to natural habitat includes: (i) go for a natural look rather than a formal one; (ii) select a limited number of plant varieties and bunch them together in drifts; (iii) plant evergreen ground covers; (iv) select plants appropriate to your climate; (v) incorporate paved surfaces and fences.

[9] There are exceptions to this rule, which take into consideration the time and space dimensions of feng shui and the personal directional and vicinity influences.

Chapter 6

Environmental assessment

A recent cartoon shows the management of a construction crew reviewing plans at a construction site. In front of them a bulldozer is knocking down mature trees and scraping the land bare of native vegetation. While pointing at the bare ground behind the dozer the project manager says, 'And over there we'll do some landscaping'.

Working *with* nature is the key to success. This means following the natural contours of the land, paying attention to the natural cycles, respecting and restoring habitat. (What a contrast to the typical project that clear-cuts the natural world and replaces it with streets named after what was removed.) Working with nature creates fewer revenge effects.

The most important reason to pay attention to initial conditions (including what we do to the land) is that the revenge effect lurks in everything we do. Research the history of a site. Design with due diligence.[1] Give thoughtful consideration to the life of a project, its programme, and its contribution to the community. Project a site into the future with a series of programmes.

A proposed programme does not stop at property lines. Think about the interconnectedness of the world—that is the essence of sustainability and of feng shui, the original science of environmental protection.

A competent feng-shui practitioner uses a general set of techniques and tools when conducting an analysis of a structure, including but not limited to the environmental assessment. More than a mere appraisal of landscaping, this inspection involves observing everything in the area, generally within a 1-km radius. 'Everything' includes geography, adjacent buildings, bioclimate, natural light and ventilation, sound, and rough estimates of the thermal levels of a structure. A more scientific version would encompass a climatic survey (temperature and relative humidity), and documentation of wind effects. These data, when plotted on a bioclimatic chart, would provide a diagnosis of an area's temperature and humidity over a particular period. It could identify whether

a particular structure is optimally oriented. Feng shui provides similar results with different methods.

Existing structures

Topography and natural features

As explained in Chapter 5, evaluation techniques involve much more than seeing symbolism in everything. 'Bad feng shui' is another way of saying environmental and personal suffering. To alleviate these issues feng-shui practitioners identify and evaluate the following components of a site.

Microclimate

Microclimate defines the distinctive climate of a small-scale area. A combination of many slightly different microclimates creates the climate for a particular area. Formed by houses, fences, vegetation, water features, and paved surfaces, microclimates create subtle but very real differences in temperatures and conditions. Urban microclimates generally trap heat and produce a sweltering environment capable of damaging plants. For example, if one area of a yard is shaded but a spot just a few meters away is in full sun, temperature differences between the two can vary by as much as 10 or 15° (see Figure 6.1).

The reflection of solar radiation by glass buildings and windows produces high albedo rates that raise temperature and make visibility difficult. Moreover, structures displaying large amounts of glass take a deadly toll on wildlife.[2] The built environment offers abundant opportunities to reduce death and misery, save resources, reduce waste, and restore damaged land (see Figure 6.2).

Feng-shui practitioners assess the amount and quality of vegetation, its arrangement, and its relation to the built environment. They examine the topography and check for water features. Nearby buildings are analysed for their effect on the site. Any wildlife or domestic animals (and their absence) are noted. Practitioners

(a)

Figure 6.1

(a) Two different microclimates. This is public housing on the south side of Chicago, Illinois (USDA photo by Ken Hammond). (b) This is an adobe house next to a field of chili peppers in Dixon, New Mexico (USDA photo by Russell Lee).

(b)

consider how a building integrates into the natural world and build a cognitive map of the site's microclimate.

Pollution

More than two million children die each year from the effects of environmental degradation. Nearly one-third of the global disease burden can be attributed to environmental problems, and more than 40 per cent of that burden falls on children under five—who comprise a mere 10 per cent of the world's population. Children run

Figure 6.2

Deceptive design: expanses of glass provide a formidable and deadly hazard to all kinds of birds, raise local temperatures, and impair visibility (photo by the author).

a disproportionate risk to global environmental problems such as climate change and loss of biodiversity.[3] These are things to think about during the design process.

'Pollution' is not limited to the following.

Visual pollution

Visual pollution includes the homogenized built environment where structures do not evolve from places or sites but are set down whole on site-planned parcels. It can include buildings and landscaping blind to a region and its seasonal cycles;[4] oversized houses slapped cheek by jowl on minimally landscaped, undersized parcels; and suburban fences tagged with graffiti, painted over, and tagged again. Although sometimes a subjective observation (the concept of 'clutter' for instance), visual pollution more typically includes lighting, urban blight, brownfields, and sinks (see Figure 6.3).

A *brownfield* defines local land, water, and air used as a disposal system by business or government. These sites often consist of a piled mass of indefinable material left indefinitely to influence the environment. They include abandoned, idled, and underused industrial and commercial facilities where

Figure 6.3

A stereotypical form of visual pollution. US Fish and Wildlife Service.

expansion or redevelopment stopped because of real or perceived environmental contamination.

Sometimes brownfields include the effects of superstore sprawl when retailers close megamalls and 'relocate' to other towns, leaving in their wake empty stores with weeds growing through cracks in the parking lot. In most cases the buildings stay shuttered because the community cannot afford to demolish them and return the land to productive use. (The National Trust for Historic Preservation claims that fully half a billion of the five billion square feet of retail space in the US sits empty and surrounded by a sea of asphalt.) See Figure 6.4.

Sprawl identifies the developed world's 'favela syndrome' (rapid urbanization and environmental problems) because it also encourages racial disparity, class stratification, and environmental degradation.[5] Robert Bullard, a sociologist who heads the

Figure 6.4

Some typical brownfields. City of Troitsk, Chelyabinsk, CIS, 2 April 1992. Photo courtesy of NASA (STS045-75-644)

Environmental Justice Resource Center at Clark Atlanta University, says *sprawl* is a kinder word than what it really is: white flight (see Figure 6.5).

Grady Clay defined *sinks* as 'places of last resort into which powerful groups in society shunt, shove, dump, and pour whatever or whomever they do not like or cannot use'.[6] Feng shui encompasses environmental justice. Any community should be planned for social equity. Today environmental racism, often practiced in the guise of smart growth, sites chemical industries, highways, garbage dumps, smelters, incinerators, and other polluting facilities in the communities of people of colour. Exclusionary and expulsive zoning methods are regularly applied. The auto reigns supreme, so that a form of transportation racism goes into effect. Laws and regulations are haphazardly enforced—especially with regards to clean air and water, parks and greenways, and affordable housing in all communities. Energy conservation is most desperately needed by the lower echelons of society, but regularly they are the ones who least benefit.

A confusing and dangerous built environment constitutes the very antithesis of feng shui. The built environment exists to create continuity so people do not have to think and analyse every movement

Figure 6.5

How sprawl looks from space: a typical American neighbourhood. Photo credit: NASA.

they make. People expect the natural world to provide a lack of continuity and require a higher level of awareness. However, if continuity is missing from an area improved for humans there is an increase in negative health effects.[7]

Noise pollution
Noise pollution is usually identified as human- and machine-generated sounds, although unique cases exist where natural sounds (including frogs, crickets, roosters, and songbirds) disturb people. Fatigue, stress, and other suffering directly related to noise pollution diminish the quality of life and create health problems. If people have the money they move. If they cannot afford to move they are left to suffer.

Lack of soundproofing creates the most tenant complaints in apartment complexes and row houses (condominiums). Thinner walls cost less, but builders never investigate the revenge effects in their designs—specifically how they affect the way sound travels from one unit to another. High-quality buildings get adequate soundproofing when developers want to retain tenants or when soundproofing is required by law. Yet enough simple, cost-effective techniques exist to install sufficient soundproofing in *all* structures. A quiet structure induces people to stay as it keeps them healthier.[8]

Air pollution

Motor vehicles constitute the biggest single source of atmospheric pollution. Sixty-five per cent of all carbon monoxide emissions come from road vehicles. Automotive fuels account for 17 per cent of global carbon dioxide releases—two-thirds as much as rainforest destruction.

Air pollution remains high in US urban areas because the average American driver spends 443h/year (the equivalent of 55 eight-hour workdays) behind the wheel and wastes an estimated US$ 72 billion a year in traffic jams. Americans also spend more on transportation than any other household expense—one-fifth of their income. Residents of sprawling communities drive three to four times as much as those living in compact, well-planned areas, plus 80 per cent of more than 115 million Americans making the daily commute drive by themselves. Adding new lanes and building new roads exacerbates revenge effects, according to studies that show increasing road capacity merely creates more traffic and more sprawl.

Buildings generate 35 per cent of US carbon dioxide emissions, 49 per cent of sulfur dioxide emissions, 25 per cent of nitrous oxide emissions, and 10 per cent of particulate emissions. Thanks to urban heat islands and the combined pollutant output of buildings and cars, higher temperatures in metropolitan areas accelerate the production of smog, escalate energy consumption due to increased air conditioning, and intensify stress, illness, and suffering. Research at the US Department of Energy at Lawrence Berkeley National Laboratories in Berkeley, California, concluded that shrinking the amount of ground-level ozone and smog could save US$ 5 billion in medical costs and lost work.[9]

Today, asthma is the most common and chronic childhood disease and it is exacerbated by urban air pollution.[10] According to the Centers for Disease Control and Prevention, asthma is the fourth leading cause of disability in kids under 18 years. Between 1980 and 1994, the prevalence of asthma increased 75 per cent overall and 74 per cent among children 5–14 years of age. From 1992 to 1999, the number of emergency hospital visits for asthma increased 36 per cent. However, environmental pollution predominantly affects people of colour. Low-income populations, minorities, and children living in inner cities suffer disproportionately from asthma. African Americans suffer asthma-related emergency hospital visits, hospitalization, and death rates three times higher than rates for whites.

Watercourses and streets

Analyse these features according to the principles examined in Chapter 5. Resolutions to problems depend on the particulars of a situation. Narrow streets slow vehicular traffic and encourage pedestrian use; this makes a neighbourhood hospitable to visitors, children, the elderly, and animals ('good feng shui').[11] Sometimes a fast-moving street provides beneficial feng shui, but that is a rare occurrence—and a judgment based solely on a case-by-case basis.

Consider street and water orientation in relation to a site. In some feng shui techniques these provide enhancements while in others their orientation is a detriment. The infamous T intersection, like the long and straight watercourse, can be a force for good if a site is constructed to capitalize on its strengths (usually sites that accommodate the T intersection are large building complexes). A residence facing a straight road, watercourse, or a T intersection typically meets with trouble because the site cannot withstand the revenge effects. Over a period of years in one southern California neighbourhood cars regularly overshot a T intersection and crashed into the fence and back yard of the house that it faced. The exasperated owner took preventive measures that any decent feng-shui practitioner would advise: he planted a massive barricade of vegetation between the intersection and the back yard wall. So far it seems to be working and, as an added bonus, it has reduced the street noise.

Topographic problems

Other items likely to be noted by a practitioner during an analysis include the slopes of hillsides and pads, the amount of land

between the back of a structure on a pad and the hillside or its retaining wall; soil conditions and erosion; cracks in the dirt, structures, water features; and the general condition of the land.

What constitutes bad feng shui can be called by any number of contemporary labels and supported by reams of data. Cut-and-fill, clear-cutting, and other large-scale engineering interventions typically create appalling environments from any number of viewpoints. In traditional feng-shui theory, misery prevails when development amputates or redirects beneficial 'dragons' and in any way impedes the natural flow of the land. Many builders think nothing of bulldozing the tops off hills or slicing hillsides in half to build subdivisions and condominium complexes. Property owners, residents, and managers are left to deal with the revenge effects of these ill-conceived designs.

Two lawsuits in 1998 on behalf of 115 northern California homeowners claimed that the concrete foundations of all homes in their subdivision were suffering alkali-silica reaction (a chemical process that expands concrete until it falls apart), the usual flooding and drainage problems associated with cut-and-fill development, inadequate and defective soils analysis, geotechnical planning and preparation shortfalls, site grading deficiencies, and a host of defective workmanship issues.

Orientation
Many buildings simply are not positioned or designed appropriately for their orientation—energy bills tend to confirm this—and feng shui provides categories that indicate additional orientation problems. A classic example is the 'waterfront' building with its front on the dry side, but there is a short list of other structures that typically frustrate and alienate their owners and occupants.

Double facing, or down mountain
The general level of suffering in this structure intensifies with the presence of water at the front. Practitioners contend that this type of building fosters professional success at the expense of relationships,

marriages, partnerships, and families. Often the solution is to add berms, big trees, buildings, or boulders at an appropriate orientation. These factors are determined during a feng-shui analysis.

Double sitting, or up mountain

The general level of suffering in this structure intensifies with the presence of a building, large tree, boulders, or berms at the back. Most practitioners insist this type of building is hard on finances but good with health and relationships. Often the solution is to add a water feature at an appropriate orientation.

Reversed

Practitioners regularly describe this type of building as inherently bad feng shui. Consensus among practitioners is that this particular type of house forms the bulk of foreclosures, but often there are other attendant miseries. In general, the reversed structure requires the most extensive environmental remedies (water and berms, large vegetation, buildings, or boulders) scaled according to their size. The period from the late 1940s to early 1960s was a particularly fruitful one for these structures. Entire US subdivisions created during the post-World War II housing boom conform to these orientations.

Up the mountain, down the river

Sometimes a structure receives additional emphasis on its problems due to the siting of rivers or fast-moving streets, plus the positioning of elevations and nearby hills or large buildings.

Native plants and animals

Few feng-shui practitioners are biologists, but they typically observe a location and evaluate its natural environment. Practitioner training reinforces the principle that, as part of the goal of harmony with nature, even the most urban location should provide sufficient vegetation and habitat. Suggested remedies should

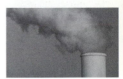

stress plants and other solutions consistent with the native species of a particular area.[12]

'Good feng shui' provides more than a catchphrase. Jamie Rappaport Clark of the US Fish and Wildlife Service noted that the habitats attracting birds in urban areas (such as parks, greenways, and tree-lined streets) improve the quality of life in any community. An improved quality of life is also good for business: services related to the presence of birds, such as bird-watching, housing, and feeding, earned an estimated US\$ 29 billion in 1996.

It is a practitioner's responsibility to suggest appropriate remedies and methods of environmental resolution. Unfortunately, some practitioners are more knowledgeable and conscientious than others. Practitioners need to form partnerships with local wildlife organizations and authorities to expand their knowledge and the solutions they offer their clients. Their websites should provide clients and the curious with links to extensive environmental information and encouragement.

Restoring habitat

Restoration is defined as the process of re-establishing a self-sustaining habitat that closely resembles a natural condition in terms of structure and function. Quality environments provide a variety of habitats (aquatic, forest, field, and edge).

Children gain the most from habitat restoration because often they are the most faithful users of open space in a neighbourhood. They prize outdoor places that enable them to explore the natural world and make use of natural materials. They do not need a big area, but wildlife habitats that work for children should be designed into a site, centrally located in residential developments, shielded by homes instead of streets, and provided social and physical safety.

Species loss occurs when development isolates small areas and expects creatures to thrive there. Too often habitat islands engulfed by homes and businesses are too small or too isolated to provide wildlife with their basic necessities. Many animals require a variety of habitat types nearby to meet their needs. The size, vegetation diversity, and interconnectedness of such islands determine the number, size, and kinds of creatures a habitat can support. The shape of a habitat patch also affects wildlife because it influences the relative amounts of habitats.

In general, circular habitats function better than angular ones. *Edge habitat* (parcels of habitat not more than several hundred meters wide) benefits only certain kinds of wildlife, usually at the expense of others.[13] *Interior habitat* provides insulation from edge effects such as noise, wind, sun, and predators—all of which are critical to species that dwell deeper in a wild area. An interior habitat begins to develop approximately 50 m from the edge of a habitat, although habitats for some species may need to be as much as 550 m from an edge.

Corridors and greenways aid wildlife and provide additional value in a developed area.[14] Maintaining and creating these systems increases their use and the likelihood that many species of wildlife will thrive.

Sustainability and 'green' issues

'Green renovation' or 'green remodelling' harmonizes with the principles of feng shui because thinking green complements traditional concepts of sustainability. A conventional home in a typical new suburb consumes more resources than necessary, diminishes the environment, and generates an enormous amount of landfill waste. The standard wood-framed home devours more than an acre of forest (as the stock of large-diameter trees has steadily declined) and creates from 3 to 7 tonnes of waste during construction.

Environmentally sound renovation saves renovation costs in its use of quality salvaged materials, decreases the amount of landfill that is normally required for construction waste, and conserves existing resources. It cuts energy costs by obtaining materials locally, lowers indoor air pollution (due to the use of lower-VOC surface finishes and fewer artificial materials for carpeting and upholstery), and safeguards the health and safety of workers and occupants through its use of less-toxic materials.[15]

Building colours should reflect native soil and plants as a general interpretation of Earth hues on a vertical plane. A renovated site should be integrated back into nature. It does not matter whether initially the nearest 'nature' is kilometers away—*what matters is that the integration occurs*. As more buildings are renovated and entire city blocks 'go native' it will be easier to identify the 'natural' environment.[16]

Textures used in renovation should also work towards the goal of integration with nature. Concrete block, stone, stucco, and wood provide symbolic variations of natural textures. At the same time, considering the amount of yin and yang at a site means selecting the appropriate textures with care to achieve an optimum ratio (in general two-thirds yang to one-third yin).

Improve local microclimates during renovation. This means using environmentally correct surface coatings on rooftops,[17] increasing (native) vegetation by rooftop gardens or other means, adding corridors and greenways when appropriate. Do not forget to apply innovative techniques to areas for parking, which are notorious heat islands that devour land. For every degree increase in heat, electricity generation rises by 2–4 per cent and smog production increases by 4–10 per cent.

Streets and parking lots constitute the largest component of urban impervious cover—for example, half of urban land in Florida is dedicated to autos and their problems, according to the Florida Conservation Foundation. Pavement now covers more than 2 per cent of the total surface area of the US, and 10 per cent of all arable land in the US.

Landscape architect Dan Kiley is credited with defining a parking lot as a 'garden for cars'—a pathetic concept, because cars are not the least bit appreciative. However, a superior solution exists and it *can* be valued by living creatures. *Green parking* refers to several techniques collectively applied to reduce the amount of impervious cover created by parking lots. A comprehensive green parking programme can effectively reduce the amount of impervious cover, help to protect local streams, save money in storm water management, and beautify a site. Techniques include setting maximums for the number of parking lots, determining average parking demand (instead of setting parking ratios to accommodate the highest hourly parking during the peak season), minimizing the dimensions of parking lot spaces, utilizing alternative pavers in overflow parking areas, creating natural areas to retain and treat storm water,[18] encouraging shared parking, and providing economic incentives for structured parking.

Green paving consists of a combination of alternative paving[19] and hardy plants that can withstand a fair amount of vehicular traffic. A successful green parking programme depends on shrinking the amount of impervious cover, and on which techniques are combined to create the 'greenest' lot. Fort Bragg in North Carolina constructed a green parking lot that reduced impervious cover by 40 per cent, increased parking by 20 per cent, and saved US$ 1.6 million—20 per cent—on construction costs over the initial conventional design. A green paving system in Auburn, Washington, consists of grass and porous structural plastic for use as a park and for overflow parking. A combination of grass and cement concrete block is also effective. Concrete blocks are laid on compacted ground and a hardy variety of grass is grown through the openings in the bricks. Mature grass is not harmed because its roots are below the edges of the bricks, which, in turn, distribute the loads of heavy vehicles.

Green parking and green paving reduce costs and the size of heat islands as they beautify and enrich the urban environment. However, at best these techniques are shortsighted sops to car addicts. Reducing and/or eliminating vehicles and their voracious need for their own 'gardens' (always at the expense of living creatures) should be the goal.[20] Studies indicate that business profits grow when cities exclude cars from their centres and provide more areas of pedestrian-only access.

Using environment to correct problems in existing buildings

For feng shui, the most important and consequential remedies involve microclimatic changes. That is why practitioners advise strategically placed water features,[21] berms, boulders, large trees, or other forms of vegetation (as previously explained in *Orientation*). A practitioner might suggest remodelling to compensate for unpromising calculations or to capitalize on a promising orientation (as in the Castle Gate technique). Whatever the remedy, it should be viewed as an opportunity to further integrate a structure into the natural world. To that end, utilize local and sustainable materials and practices whenever possible. Strive to create wildlife habitat as part of the feng-shui remedy and receive additional therapeutic benefits (see Chapter 7).

Bare land

Twice as many people buy an existing home than a new home primarily because of the character of neighbourhoods. An established neighbourhood shows whether it is successful and properly located.

Without experience, the latest space syntax tools, or an adept feng-shui practitioner, it is more difficult to tell whether a new community will share these features.

Most buildings are built for a particular market at a particular time. Developers and designers can misjudge a market or follow a design philosophy that fluctuates as quickly as any fad. Because these buildings cannot change like the market they are quickly dated and reduced to functional obsolescence.[22]

Generally, poor orientation and fit of house to land and climate also make these buildings quite expensive to light, heat, and cool. Inferior landscaping choices waste excessive amounts of water and create environmental revenge effects.[23] Many ordinary construction materials produce poor indoor air quality, which can lead to health problems.

Topography and natural features

Developing a new neighbourhood in the conventional sense involves considering what to bulldoze and what to keep. Developing yet another 'bedroom community' splinters what is left of any open space and wildlife habitat, and/or removes yet more productive farmland and forest area from use.

What stages of construction are affected by building green? Site planning, design, the construction process, materials and specifications, foundations, structure and framing, sheathing and exterior finish, insulation, roofing, doors and windows, floor coverings, paints, coatings and adhesives, exterior finish and trim. Although ethical principles inherent in feng shui correspond to sustainability principles, they may not be workable for everyone. Some may have to be forced by economic necessity and/or legislation to comply with these ideas and techniques.

During the planning process, exercise due diligence toward the natural world. Obtain the advice of biologists and other local habitat experts on primary areas for preservation. A feng-shui practitioner can assist in siting a development with the flow of the land, and in minimizing the revenge effects associated with development (including, but not limited to workmanship, construction accidents, fires, crimes, and health hazards). A practitioner can also advise on what orientations and layouts would be most beneficial for the widest range of occupants—or, if this is a custom development, a practitioner can provide additional detailed information on what clients require as optimum conditions.

As you begin the design and development processes you will also want to consider the following issues.

Pollution

Any new construction affects the environment. Feng-shui advice can help, but it cannot eliminate this effect. Green building and environmental assessment are essential and currently provide the only way to diminish pollution.

Watercourses and streets

Resist the temptation to turn a natural local water feature into a cement pond or otherwise destroy it. Let feng shui aid in analysing the position of the water dragon and redesigning its flow, if needed, to accentuate the good features of water and the site. The presence of this feature delights humans and wildlife. A natural watercourse adjusts a microclimate's air circulation, relative humidity, temperature, and wildlife habitat. Piping water underground as a nuisance degrades the environment and creates bad feng shui.

Good feng shui for roadways and streets corresponds to good civic design and planning, with certain caveats.

Positioning and average speed

Streets are like streams and rivers; revenge effects occur if the orientation is not appropriate for all structures near them. Cul-de-sacs can be good for all houses, or only one or two on the entire block—it is all in how they are designed. Government buildings can benefit from appropriate use of T intersections, while some unfortunate suburban homeowner may find one car after another swimming in his pool because they fail to negotiate the stop. Residential streets whose broad design encourages speeding create fear, animosity, and heartache in residents—fear for the lives of their children and pets, animosity against those who feel confident enough to use the street as a racetrack, and heartache in those who suffer tragedy as a result of insensitive design.

Feeder and connector streets

Feng-shui principles dictate that a good environment aids the flow of life and by extension perhaps the transition to larger and faster thoroughfares. Facilitate a new development's integration with public transportation services and provide safe transitional environments for pedestrians and the natural world—sprawl is notoriously unfriendly to public transit, bicycles, and pedestrians.

Topography
Was the site predetermined by the developer or by setback limits?
Consider all possible revenge effects of development decisions (all the more critical in these increasingly litigious times). The natural environment—not the built one—is of paramount importance.

Are local features cherished?
Does the site preserve and enhance the local microclimate—the flow of the land, natural water features, existing boulders, swales, and natural rock outcroppings? Does it preserve and/or enhance wildlife habitats? Resist the temptation to create a Disney Desert or similar travesty. Turn difficult slopes along with wetlands, canyon bottoms, flood plains, cliffs, buttes, and other sensitive areas into biological reservoirs and recreation areas. Natural runoff floodways and wetlands constitute high-energy ecological reserves that produce more than any farmland.[24]

How does a structure relate to a site?
Is the structure integrated into the natural flow of the land? Is it destined to be dropped on a cut-and-fill pad in a landscape ravaged by backhoes and earthmovers, devoid of wildlife and natural beauty? Is the natural world incorporated into the building's design, or is this a stereotypical urban geography blind to the planet—an egotistical CAD fantasy?

Orientation
How should a building sit on a lot?
Take advantage of orientations to maximize comfort and minimize energy consumption. Protect orientations that extend the seasons and work with the land. (Turning one house 90° saved the occupants more than 30 per cent on their energy bills.) Determine the direction of prevailing breezes and adjust window designs to take advantage of them. Calculate what the year of construction will build into the house and adjust the orientation accordingly (more on that in Chapter 7).

Sustainability and 'green' issues

Green building for most developers means rethinking business and customers. When rating the importance of energy efficiency, resource conservation, and indoor air quality on a scale of 1 to 5 (with 5 being most important), buyers give each issue a significantly higher mark than builders do.

One annual green building survey[25] underscores the dissimilar mindsets of buyers and builders. Builders on average fail to satisfy their customers' passion for environmentally healthy homes. Buyers want new homes that are energy-efficient, resource-efficient, and healthy—and they are willing to pay more for these benefits than builders assume they will.

Eight in ten consumers surveyed in 2001 said that new homes do not meet their sustainability demands. Nine out of ten respondents said that energy-efficient features in a new home are 'extremely' or 'very important'. Six in ten respondents said the use of certified, sustainably harvested lumber should be standard in new homes. Eight in ten consumers prefer a home that is built without using old-growth trees.

Builders consistently underestimate the value of green building features to their customers. For example, little more than half of the builders who were surveyed in 2001 regularly use formaldehyde-free insulation in the homes they build, yet 85 per cent of buyers say they want this kind of insulation. Seventy-three per cent of buyers want low-VOC paint to be standard in new homes, but a mere 58 per cent of builders regularly use these paints.

Using the environment to correct problems

So you did not call in the feng-shui practitioner until the slabs were poured and now she is telling you that the orientations are all wrong. You want your project to sell and for people to be happy with your work. What can she do to make this happen?

If you created a neighbourhood of homes with orientation problems, adjust the microclimate for each structure according to the

locations and orientations provided by the feng-shui practitioner. Install the appropriate features as part of the finishing process or landscaping. These items do not add substantially to your costs and they substantially increase the occupants' happiness with what you have built.

If you created a commercial complex with an orientation problem, work with the practitioner to resolve the issues. Adjusting the microclimate may be enough, but the size of the complex determines the scale of the adjustments that need to be made.

You may find that what is required to remedy the site is beyond the scope of your project. In that case, learn from the practitioner what revenge effects are likely to occur as a result of the inherent problems in the complex and see what small changes can be made. Sometimes small remedies advantageously placed can make enough of a difference.

Notes

[1] According to one firm, due diligence consists of a discovery process that identifies latent defects in function design, such as threats and opportunities (http://www.spaceanalytics.com/desd.htm).

[2] Estimated bird deaths each year due to reflective glass and glass windows range from 100 to 900+ million according to Dr Daniel Klem of Muhlenberg College. From 1968 to 1998, more than 26000 migrating birds died crashing into Chicago's McCormick Place Convention Center during spring and fall migration. These numbers represent a small fraction of the bird fatalities that occur every year due to windows, temporary blindness caused by artificial lighting, and structures such as microwave and television towers. One 309-m tower near Tallahassee, Florida, killed 42386 birds of 190 species from 1955 to 1980. A 306-m tower in Eau Claire, Wisconsin, killed 121560 birds of 123 species from 1957 to 1994.

[3] See UNICEF, UNEP, and WHO (2002).

[4] The eastern third of the US consists of primarily wet landscape with trees and grass. The Western US generally receives less than 11 in. of rain each year. Yet, urban design rarely differentiates between the two climates. This contributes to the homogeneity of US urban areas deplored by experts and communities alike.

[5] Research conducted by the National Wildlife Federation discovered that sprawl imperils 188 of the 286 California species listed under the US Endangered Species Act. The National Wetlands Inventory, conducted every 10 years by the US Fish and Wildlife Service,

established that 644 000 acres of wetlands were lost between 1986 and 1997. Thirty per cent of wetland loss—the single largest contribution—came as the result of new development (National Wildlife Federation, 2001).

[6] See Clay (1973, p. 143).

[7] See Brown (2001).

[8] See Melamed et al. (2001).

[9] See Rosenfeld et al. (1996).

[10] On summer days with high pollution children with asthma are 40 per cent more likely to suffer asthma attacks compared with days with average pollution levels. Increases in air pollution levels in the summer months are associated with a rise in the daily number of hospital emergency room visits by elderly people. The levels of ozone and particulate matter linked in the study with increased ER visits were well below current US air quality standards (Delfino et al., 1997; Thurston et al., 1997).

[11] Pedestrian fatality rates are higher in the US for people of colour, according to the US Department of Transportation. In 1997, more than 5000 pedestrians were struck and killed by cars—over two-thirds of the victims were men. Walking is 36 times more dangerous than driving.

[12] Introducing non-native species is against feng-shui principles.

[13] Most wildlife inhabiting edges are considered generalist species.

[14] A corridor is a connective landscape that unites habitat islands. An effective wildlife corridor is wide enough to provide food, water, and shelter for an animal as it moves through.

[15] The Green Building Council is the foremost US coalition of leaders from across the building industry working to promote buildings that are environmentally responsible, profitable, and healthy places to live and work. The council's LEED Green Building Rating System for Existing Buildings consists of performance standards for the sustainable operation of existing buildings. The LEED-EB criteria cover building operations and systems upgrades in existing buildings where the majority of interior or exterior surfaces remain unchanged.

[16] For some ideas see Bonham et al. (2002).

[17] In countries around the sun-baked Mediterranean people are directed by law to whitewash their roofs after the rainy season ends. Reflective roofs diminish the effects of heat islands.

[18] Bioretention areas are landscaping features adapted to provide on-site treatment of storm water runoff. They are commonly located in parking lot islands on small sites or within small pockets of residential land in highly urbanized settings, and use approximately 5 per cent of the area that drains to them. Surface runoff flows into shallow, landscaped depressions that incorporate many of the pollutant removal mechanisms found in forest eco-systems. Natural areas to retain storm water help meet storm water management and

landscaping requirements as they minimize maintenance costs. Although few studies exist on the pollutant removal rates of bioretention areas, they are estimated to be as efficient as a dry swale, which eliminates 91 per cent of total suspended solids, 67 per cent of total phosphorous, 92 per cent of total nitrogen, and 80–90 per cent of metals.

[19] Some alternative pavers include gravel, cobbles, wood mulch, brick, grass pavers, turf blocks, natural stone, pervious concrete, and porous asphalt.

[20] Approximately one million animals per day are killed on US roads. Declines in the numbers of endangered animals can, in part, be attributed to highway deaths.

[21] A general rule of thumb is water volume at 5 per cent of the square meterage or square footage of the structure, rounded off to the higher amount of litres or gallons.

[22] http://www.spaceanalytics.com.

[23] A government 'hit list' of invasive trees, aquatic plants, and herbs can be found at www.nps.gov/plants/alien/.

[24] A salt marsh of Spartina grass produces 3500 g of biomass per square metre each year. Farmland can produce a mere 1700 g from growing sugarcane, 400 g from growing maize, and 350 g from growing wheat.

[25] Conducted by the Cahners Residential Group and Professional Builder, Housing Zone, E-One, Panasonic, Willamette, the Wood Promotion Network, CertainTeed, and USGBC.

Chapter 7

Human factors

The innate human need for particular environments and views

People wonder why doctors' offices and other stressful locations often contain fish tanks. Studies of dentists' offices show that watching an aquarium before a procedure enables patients to behave more compliantly during procedures, to recover more quickly, and to experience less pain and trauma.[1] Other research shows that watching an aquarium can significantly lower people's blood pressure below the resting level—and it does not matter whether their blood pressure is naturally normal or high. People constantly exposed to stress suffer immune system dysfunction yet views of nature aid our immune system and help us regain health quickly[2] (see Figure 7.1).

Talking to an animal lowers blood pressure and heart rate more than talking to human familiars—in fact, as most people with pets know, the mere presence of animals increases the level of social interaction among humans.[3] Long-standing advice for single men includes borrowing a friend's dog as a way to meet women, because women, in general, are friendlier to people with a dog. Many people consider animals as kin, and animals elicit speech from people. Women tend to stop to pet a dog and strike up a conversation. The increased use of animals as assisted therapists in the health-care industry is the direct result of research showing how animals help us heal and increase our quality of life.[4]

Figure 7.1

Pictures like this lower human blood pressure and heart rate. US Fish and Wildlife Service. Photo by Gary M. Stolz.

Extended exposure to window views of nature by hospital patients and prison inmates also provides far-reaching effects. Surgical patients with a view of greenery have shorter hospital stays, receive fewer negative comments in nurse's notes, and apparently experience fewer postoperative complications. Patients forced to stare at a blank wall need more potent and more frequent pain medications, while people with views of foliage need only minor pain relievers. Similarly, studies of prison inmates provided with views of scenery showed they had fewer sick calls and less health-related symptoms of stress such as headaches and digestive problems.

A Swedish hospital with psychiatric patients studied the effects of environment for 15 years. Patients responded positively to wall art with natural content but not to abstracts and other modern forms of art. The research indicated that what prompted patients to attack staff verbally and physically—and even pull items down and smash them, a rarity for patients considered nonviolent and passive—was abstract and chaotic content. In the 15 years of research, no patient ever complained about or attacked a picture depicting nature.[5]

We may try to shut out the natural world, but the sense of beauty it imparts to humans affects us more profoundly than we realize. Our love of nature has been defined as 'love with feeling and thinking'.[6] People stuck in offices all day but provided access to a window with a view of greenery suffer less stress and take fewer sick days. (I once took a tour of a corporation that stuck its artists in the windowless basement of the building; they retaliated by hanging posters depicting a natural view through a window. People in behavioural studies and postoccupation studies behave the same way.[7]) You can 'bliss out' watching birds, other animals, and water. The effects of studying natural scenes apparently induce in humans feelings not unlike those found in Zen meditation.

None of this information is new to those familiar with E.O. Wilson's Biophilia Hypothesis, which seeks to understand the human affinity for living things. (A corollary, Biophobia, explains why we and

our fellow primates tend to exhibit similar negative reactions to snakes and bugs, and why some people love technology more than the natural world.) In an accumulation of books and studies, proponents of this theory see a correlation between the natural world that humans evolved in and the optimal state of human well-being. Scientists have also documented the debilitating effects of a world devoid of nature or provided in diminished levels, and humans' corresponding level of mental and emotional distress (see Figure 7.2).

Notice the qualifier 'the natural world that humans evolved in'. The natural world that we long for and need for our continued health looks nothing like the places where most of us live. It is a world that takes us back before the Industrial Revolution (at the latest). Consider the ominous implications of these data, especially when crime is considered a largely urban pathology. A few studies suggest that most mental health cases live in urban areas. Some experts link the escalating trend of events like the massacre at Columbine High and workplace shootings with the marginalizing landscapes of suburbia and a rising tide of mental illness. The increase of mental illness appears to coincide with industralization, especially urbanization, and is likely biological.[8] We may have

jure 7.2

ımans are hard-wired to want trees that look like the ones
r distant ancestors encountered in Africa. US Fish and
dlife Service. Photo by Gary M. Stolz.

proof that humanity is going slowly mad and self-destructing due to
our way of building.

Viewshed, human nature, and feng shui

Humans require natural views of plants and animals for mental and
emotional health. Studies also suggest we need nature around
us as a restorative and to stimulate our higher creative functions.
(Anecdotal evidence links walks in a park or other natural
settings with ideas that eventually led their creators to receive
Nobel prizes.) Our need for the natural world is truly ancient.
Evidence from Olduvai Gorge and other archeological digs in eastern
Africa indicate that our distant ancestors made the first efforts to
achieve the same surroundings that we desire. Early hominids
generally located their camps at the edge of water. They positioned
themselves with water to their front and a hillside, cave, or other
protective natural feature at their back.

Millions of years separate the Neolithic beginnings of feng shui from
our ancestors in Africa, but key features remain the same: water in
the front, a hill or mountain at the back. Techniques merely increased
in sophistication between the time of African hominids and
Neolithic Chinese. Numbers and instrumentation provided additional
analytical techniques. People learned to improve the landscape so
that it provided the by-now 'sacred' features, always with the
intended goal of integrating humanity into what is Naturally So.

When Christian missionaries arrived in China in the nineteenth
century they marvelled at the beauty and fertility of the land, even
as they denounced as 'pagan superstition' the ancient techniques
that provided people with their rich environment. A similar situation
occurred during the Chinese Revolution and when the Communist
Party assumed the reins of government in the People's Republic.
Mao Zedong, whose hero was Qin Shihuang, the unifier of China,
felt little love toward the ancient Chinese way of doing things. He did
everything in his power to abolish the old ways and people's senti-
ments towards them. His government used repression, propaganda,

utopian promises, and censorship to achieve its ends. What occurred in China, as the result of his policies, shows the profound connection between abuse of nature and abuse of people.

Mao disdained scientific study and principles. He prohibited farmers to continue with traditional and sustainable methods of farming, banned 'superstitious and feudal' sustainable practices (including feng shui) because of their age and traditions, and instituted nationwide programmes to eradicate birds and other wildlife. Although deforestation and other environmental degradation occurred in Imperial China, postrevolutionary China provided a much more cohesive state with unprecedented opportunities for wholesale environmental destruction. In the end it has achieved such success in remoulding the face of China that it actually threatens human survival. Today, China provides one-tenth the per-capita land resources of the US.[9]

Western traditions never extolled the urban environment as idyllic—cities for the most part provided a hotbed of disease and squalid conditions and were even expected to be that way. Westerners have been taught for centuries how to look at cities interiors and landscape. Because we cannot see the real landscape anymore, our primary reactions to the wasteland around us consist of stress and an indefinable malaise.

The work of researchers such as R. M. Nesse suggests that negative emotional states like fear, depression, and anxiety represent urgings by our embodied mind to 'attend to the situation at hand'.[10] Current generations let the next pay for their carelessness—in rising violence and mental distress.[11] We know something is 'not quite right' but we do not know what it is—or how to fix it. Some modern authorities accuse Americans of addressing these concerns with trivialities in design and place (such as clutter, perhaps?). Anti-anxiety medicines and tranquilizers can relax us, but they do not work as quickly as looking at a natural scene. People who receive training in a self-relaxation technique can become more relaxed than any current medication makes possible simply by combining self-relaxation with natural views.[12]

The cost of creating a positive living and working environment does not significantly differ from the cost of creating an oppressive one. Moreover, the bulk of scientific studies overwhelmingly conclude that healthy human environs require the same features advised by feng shui practitioners for millennia.

Environmental features

Curvilinear and rectangular visual contours or edges

Humans require soft, vague shapes and edges, and precise, definite shapes and edges in proportions resembling those expressed in yin yang theory. Geometrical design in the Western sense cannot supply what Jiahua Wu calls 'agreeable surprise' or even delight, unless the buildings are based on timeless forms of construction and their fractal nature. Differences between Western and Chinese gardens provide a glaring point of comparison. Western gardens dominate the natural world. Lineaments are mapped onto nature or at least extended out from the building. Nature serves as a frame to structure. Reflective pools mirror buildings, not aspects of nature. For Chinese, beginning with the site and its orientation, gardens and buildings are part of nature and humans blend into nature.

Buildings in the shape of squares and rectangles, ovals and circles evoke that timeless quality, provide ecological efficiency, and thus repeat in ancient and traditional habitation.[13] Consider also the Chinese concept of the 'taste of heaven'—a *taste* in the sense not of fashion or style, but of the infinite expression of deep artistic needs in a setting that reveres and represents natural forms. In contrast, much of modern architecture creates stress and misery, especially in its widespread hostility to archaeological building forms. Factor in the absence of wildlife and vegetation, and you have the typically wretched urban viewshed.

Wildlife

People need animals and wildlife, yet wildlife today exists solely by our sufferance. All but 3 per cent of Earth's biomass—including wild

Figure 7.3

Humans are hard-wired to be at their best in the company of animals. US Fish and Wildlife Service. Photo by Gary M. Stolz.

animals and vegetation—are under direct control of humans. Our misery has plenty of company (see Figure 7.3).

Returning balance to the world requires work on everyone's part, beginning with the restoration of habitat. Promote rooftop gardens and greenways, backyard wilderness, and every conceivable form of habitat renewal. When the wild things come, observe and learn to live with them by *their* rules—strive to fit in with what is Naturally So.

Landscaping and vegetation

First, we need to let the volumes of environmental data speak for themselves. Then, we need to cultivate the ability to 'see in between' our viewshed stereotypes and dogma. Some viewsheds found in feng shui seem to relate to those in Chinese painting (*shan-shui*), although feng shui uses far more orientations and calculations involved. The viewsheds from Chinese painting according to Jiahua Wu consist of *high-far, deep-far*, and *level-far*.[14]

High-far

This describes a combination of great height and distance. Eye-level viewing is intentionally placed very low. Using imagination with this viewshed creates a sense of reverence for nature that symbolizes high morality. (Think of Ansel Adams' photographs of Joshua Tree, Glacier National Park, and the face of Half Dome.) A 'guest hill' (salient landscape feature) that is high and far is auspicious (see Figure 7.4).

Figure 7.4

El Capitan as an example of *high-far*. US Fish and Wildlife Service. Photo by Gary M. Stolz.

Deep-far

This viewshed presents a means of discovery and exploration through different layers and perspectives. It promotes the use of human imagination by encouraging the creation of personal 'messages' received from intense observations of nature. *Deep-far* communicates a complex scene of layers and depths that suggests ranked, intricate qualities. It includes overhead surveying from a distance and shifting viewpoints. Complex images and spatial depth are built by careful observation and representation that can take a step beyond the real scenery and potentially move into visionary, even mystical, areas. The popularity of 'vacations in paradise' shows just how important the *Deep-far* viewshed is to our imaginations and well-being.

Consider the diverse, multilayered plant life of a rainforest. Studies show that people who are physically ill or depressed, along with children and the elderly, gravitate toward spaces that offer layers of vegetation as refuge. A guest hill that is close and small is not auspicious.

Level-far

This viewshed describes seeing from a normal, albeit modest, position. An observer receives images and composes at a typical eye level, but with wider scope and distance. Horizontal emphasis provides intimate, smooth, and familiar scenery—exactly the 'savanna-like conditions' described in Biophilia studies (see Figure 7.5). This deceptively simple viewshed contains enormous potential for depth and intensity. In a comparatively small space, someone can depict complete awareness and reveal profound feelings or moods. A guest hill that is far and faces the sitting mountain is auspicious.

Figure 7.5

A perfect example of *level-far* and savanna-like conditions in the East African Rift Zone. USGS Media for Science. Photo by Gordon Davies, courtesy of Celia Nyamweru, St Lawrence University, Canton, New York.

Figure 7.6

Jenny Lake in Grand Teton National Park, Wyoming, showing water features that appeal to humans. US Fish and Wildlife Service. Photo by Craig Rieben.

Additional viewsheds require compass readings and calculations to determine suitability.

Aquatic habitat

Humans, and especially young children, prefer and enjoy natural settings with water features. The only settings with water that generally create dismay are those that contain polluted water or water that indicates a judged set of risks, such as stormy seas. People who prefer to be challenged by nature tend to be risk-inclined young males (see Figure 7.6).

Figure 7.7

Trains and bumper-to-bumper traffic on their way to the Great Wall, People's Republic of China, in 1979. National Oceanic and Atmospheric Administration. Photo by George Saxton, NESDIS, NOAA.

Absence or inconspicuousness of artificial features (autos, buildings, signage, power lines—intrusions from the technological and commercial worlds)

People across cultural, national, and age boundaries prefer a natural landscape that hides technological intrusions. Nigerians dislike landscapes ravaged by the activities of oil exploration. Most Americans disapprove of oil exploration in the Arctic National Wilderness and despise clear-cut sections of forest. People shun viewsheds bristling with antennae, power lines, and other technology. Traditional principles of feng shui also stress concealment and de-emphasis of artificial features with enhancement of the natural world (see Figure 7.7).

Interior features

Live plants

Humans prefer natural scenes with greenery over any built views. Time and again we will choose the vista of a weed-filled, vacant lot

Figure 7.8

A lovely walk on the island of Yap. National Oceanic and Atmospheric Administration. Photo by Dr James P. McVey, NOAA Sea Grant Program.

over all except the most romanticized urban settings (such as the skyline of New York). Sad to say, the mass of the most luxurious forest is far exceeded by the sheer mass of buildings at the centre of any city. Our health and that of the planet depend on reversing that equation (see Figure 7.8).

Harmonious colour schemes

'Colour follows content', admonished Chinese painting masters. Natural use of colour, applied as nature designed, is what humans prefer. We want our built environments to echo the palette of nature because humans are tuned to the structure of colour in the natural world. Natural colours such as those in trees, lakes, and water are the colours we best remember. Our brains and bodies retain a biological expectation of particular objects exhibiting certain colours.[15] These and other visual connectors reinforce our feelings of safety. When our expectations for these items are not fulfilled their absence can create fear, depression, and anxiety.

Figure 7.9

A natural setting. National Oceanic and Atmospheric Administration. Photo by Dr James P. McVey, NOAA Sea Grant Program.

Visual access to natural settings

Look out any window and what do you see? How do you feel about it? Chances are that you gravitate to any view with a natural setting. Our longing for greenery and wildlife is quintessentially human and part of our genetic heritage. The trick in modern society is to build up the natural world and conceal or otherwise cover the artificial world. To do otherwise is to risk madness (see Figure 7.9).

Notes

1 See Ulrich (1993, p. 105).

2 See Ulrich (1993, p. 105).

3 See Heerwagen and Orians (1993, pp. 180, 185).

4 See Heerwagen and Orians (1993, p. 181).

[5] See Ulrich (1993, pp. 105–6).

[6] See Wu (1995, p. 25).

[7] See Heerwagen and Orians (1993, p. 166).

[8] See Torrey and Miller (2002).

[9] See Shapiro (2001, p. 197).

[10] The tenth most prescribed drug from the top 200 prescribed drugs in 2001 was Xanax, an anxiety relieving drug. The figures were based upon more than 3.1 billion prescriptions. (Data furnished by NDC Health; http://www.rxlist.com.)

[11] See Brown (1999). Every year, 5000 Americans between the ages of 15 and 24 commit suicide. It is the third leading cause of death for 15–24 year olds. The suicide rate is climbing—tripling since 1950 for males and more than doubling for females. From 1980 to 1996, the suicide rate for black males between the ages of 15 and 19 jumped more than 100 per cent. It is a public health crisis, and no one knows why.

[12] See Ulrich (1993, pp. 116–17).

[13] See Taylor (1983).

[14] See Wu (1995, pp. 130–1).

[15] Wichmann et al. (2002).

Chapter 8

Crime and its relation to the environment

What has feng shui got to do with it?

If you want to design an area featuring high crime, high vacancy and—ultimately—utter despoliation, design a modernistic, mini-malist high-rise with no semiprivate areas, no building entries facing streets or parking, and use 'pubic greenery' techniques of landscaping. Do not forget to include streets that encourage speeding and high levels of through-traffic.

Conventional wisdom and crime fighters say that vegetation promotes crime by concealing criminals and their activities. Following that logic, then, the most barren stretches of metropolitan areas should be crime-free—yet crime grids repeatedly demonstrate this is not the case. In fact, graffiti taggers studied in one California city *preferred* open areas devoid of landscaping.

In Chicago, a few years ago, a study of nearly 100 inner-city buildings again challenged the conventional crime-fighting wisdom. This study examined the relationship between vegetation and crime statistics in one poor neighbourhood over a lengthy period. Buildings near high levels of vegetation experienced 52 per cent fewer total crimes, 48 per cent fewer property crimes, and 56 per cent fewer violent crimes than buildings surrounded by little vegetation.[1] An earlier study also concluded that people living near trees and other vegetation reported better relations with their neighbours and less violence than other people living nearby whose buildings were surrounded by concrete. Unthreatening natural environments lower our stress levels and lift our emotional states—even if we are not stressed.[2]

Reducing crime may be as simple as adequate sunlight, open space, and plant and animal life. Designers have to get the rhythm of open and closed spaces just right, because closed spaces too densely packed and high reduce airflow, areas for vegetation, and access to sunlight—all of which make us uneasy because we instinctively know they are overrunning the natural environment.[3] Research indicates that vegetation changes our responses to an urban street—our opinions become more positive.[4]

Figure 8.1

The housing philosophy defeated by scientific studies. Poster for the New York City Housing Authority dated 20 October 1936. Work Projects Administration Poster Collection of the Library of Congress.

Study after study reinforce feng shui's requirement to assimilate humans and their buildings into the natural world. Now combine these revelations with the controversial concept of *defensible space*, which analyses and reforms housing into more natural circumstances. The deceptively simple methods used for defensible space achieve dramatic results in crime prevention and eradication. As if lifting quotes from a feng-shui testimonial, people can see for themselves how restructuring the physical layout of their community can profoundly improve their world.[5]

Modern architecture can be a repressive and brutal environment that provides little or no humanity or safety for occupants or visitors. Consider the well-known fates of modern-style buildings in public assisted housing (see Figure 8.1). People refused to live in these structures because they were visibly oppressive—eventually they left because of the appallingly high rate of crime. Most of these ambitious buildings never were used the way they were envisioned

YORK CITY
ING AUTHORITY
O VISGUERA MAYOR
ON WPOST COMM

in concept sketches, primarily because the architects knew so little about the intended occupants—they simply assumed they were people like themselves. Nearly all of these terrifying modern structures have been demolished in favour of building designs that demonstrate positive effects on human behaviour.

What seems to differ between crime-plagued housing and safe housing comes down to the size of a project and the number of units that share common entries. In the end, treating government housing projects and neighbourhoods more like villages and hamlets (that is, traditional housing) seems to work.

Consider the environment just outside the front door, day and night activities, and passages. A family's maintenance of a territory shrinks proportionally as the number of families who share maintenance increase. In a complex where many people share the same space, no one feels they can lay claim to maintenance—eventually no one does. High-rise housing projects where many families share the same entrance foster crime, primarily because funds do not exist for the watchful eyes of resident superintendents, door monitors, and elevator operators. Humans need to feel they are among neighbours and share visually accessible common ground. Garden apartments, row houses (condominiums), and walkup buildings all create defensible space. Private entrances shared by one or two families ensure safety and build community.

Someone sharing a floor with another family takes more interest in their well-being than if several families share the same entry. Substantial evidence indicates that assigning grounds (except for the streets and sidewalks) to individual families lowers the crime rate, dramatically increases the occupancy rate, and enables residents to experience a surge of neighbourhood pride.

Defining space is important for many animals, including humans. Residents need the ability to exert control over their environs (as in Jane Jacobs' oft-quoted remark that 'the windows have eyes'). We do become our brother's keeper when we understand what territory is 'ours' to claim. People whose windows and entrances face the street consider themselves accountable for what happens within

the semiprivate areas in their view. The ability to see through parks in neighbourhood housing enables residents to keep an eye on 'their' open space. People using a park facility may require active and passive use along with their need to see from one activity area into another. Play areas and paths need to be carefully marked and well-lighted. Ball game courts and public garden areas need good separation.

Small is beautiful and traditional in neighbourhoods because a small neighbourhood increases interaction, the sense of belonging, and feelings of safety and optimism. Limiting auto access and keeping streets narrow enables residents to feel that they—not passing cars—control their streets. Children play safely and traffic is restricted to people who actually have a reason for being there, which helps residents monitor activity and prevent crime. Conversely, the wider streets are in residential areas, the more it is likely that drivers will exceed the speed limit and the less it is likely that they will know their neighbours.[6]

The appearance of 'portal markers' (indicators such as gates or plantings at the entrance to a neighbourhood) signals to motorists that they are entering a different kind of street. The markers elicit a specific range of emotional responses, but all send a reminder to visitors that they are entering the streets of a close-knit community and should behave appropriately.

Notes

[1] See Coley et al. (1997) and Kuo (2001).

[2] See Ulrich (1993, p. 113).

[3] See Morrish and Brown (1994, p. 34).

[4] See Ulrich (1993, p. 103).

[5] See Newman (1996).

[6] See Duany et al. (2000, pp. 70–1).

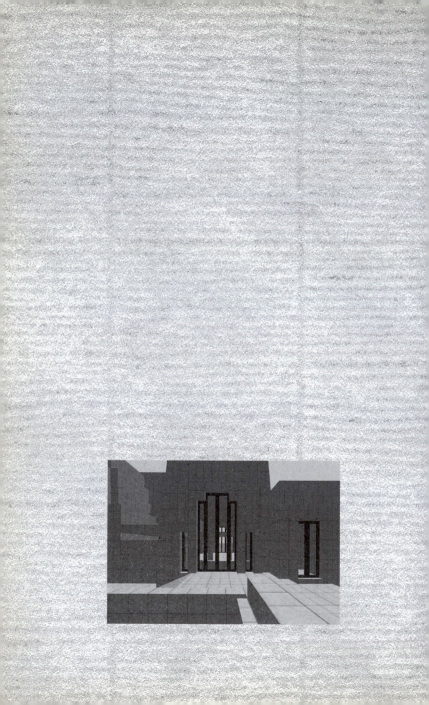

Chapter 9

Structures

*P*erhaps if we baby-proofed our homes we would lead happier and safer lives. After all, a house with no sharp corners, stairs, and other nasty surprises sounds like a pretty nice place to live. Baby-proofing might represent the fundamental feng-shui approach to housing. It certainly cannot hurt.

Traditional housing encompasses a very short list of shapes that constitute ecologically efficient forms—easy to heat and cool, to enlarge, and to remodel. They may not be glamorous but they do provide more spiritual and physical comfort than many modern structures. Because these shapes are also to some extent 'hard-wired' into our genetic makeup we can experience more profound relationships with them than, say, an octagonal shape or the infamous 'California jog' with its jagged and odd angles. People who wonder why they do not feel at home in a particular structure should discover the shape that *does* make them feel at home (see Figure 9.1).

Basics

Feng-shui principles for structures encourage the following design choices.

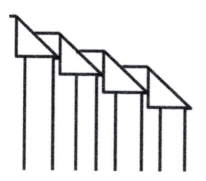

Figure 9.1

It is not a bug, it is a feature! The infamous 'California jog' as a diagram.

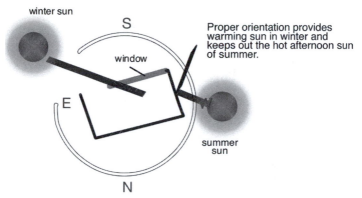

winter sun

S

window

Proper orientation provides warming sun in winter and keeps out the hot afternoon sun of summer.

E

summer sun

N

Figure 9.2

Structures designed for the local climate use less energy and provide more comfort to occupants.

Safety

Like baby-proofing, this principle assumes that everyone needs a house they can navigate comfortably in the dark or with their eyes closed—no odd angles, weird abutments, and no surprising drops or stairs. Any structure that you are afraid to let a toddler explore or to invite a senior citizen over for a visit is not good feng shui for anyone. Structures that feature a series of odd angles (like the California jog) raise stress levels and provide little or nothing in return.

Comfort

A home should *feel* homey—safe, trustworthy, quiet, and secure. No one needs to hear their neighbours' romantic escapades, incessant arguments, or obnoxious children (nor should they have to endure *yours*). A home that shields you and others from noise benefits everyone's stress levels and retains occupants longer. Insulated walls reduce energy costs and increase comfort levels with minimal effort. Natural lighting keeps people happy and productive. Designing for the local climate makes a structure energy efficient (see Figure 9.2). Small, cozy homes are universally cherished and one aspect of sustainable design (see Figure 9.3).

Figure 9.3

Small is beautiful, sustainable, and efficient when it comes to home design. In this case, the home is a yurt made of felt. From a model in DesignWorkshop Lite.

Nature first

Traditional housing has succeeded where most modern housing has not because it relies on creature comforts for a nominal investment. Modern interpretations of the old styles provide similar benefits with the advantages of some newer technologies like solar panels. But for the most part any new sustainable structures have learnt from the successes of our ancestors and expanded on their ideas.

Imagine building a subdivision into the side of a hill and using the roof of each house for green parking. Not only does this technique effortlessly keep the houses at an optimum temperature the year round, it attains the goal of integrating them into the environment. You can see a house only if you walk down a flight of natural-looking stairs next to a parking area. The view, of course, is spectacular— and so is the neighbours', and that of anyone else who passes by. In fact, if there were not any parked cars they might not necessarily think there were houses in the area. Imagine the difference in people's lives if entire towns were constructed this way.

Construction

If there is a time to plant and a time to reap, then there is a time to build and a time to occupy. While you can consult the stars or take a psychic reading, another idea might be to investigate the calculations used by feng-shui practitioners. The optimal time for construction can mean all the difference between cost overruns, labour disputes, jobsite injuries, and other development woes. Somehow feng-shui formulae can determine the likely revenge effects of a particular construction date coupled with the design and the site. For prospective buyers, these calculations can uncover the problems literally built into a home and how they can affect occupants. The calculations also establish whether a house is a good match for people and suggest occupation dates that mitigate revenge effects. Traditional feng shui simplifies house-hunting because it facilitates the selection of homes that are right for particular people.

Clients find houses that they like and send a practitioner out for a simple yes or no analysis: is it good for them or not? Based on information gathered from the property the practitioner can tell clients a great deal more about a house than a realtor may feel like divulging. This could be something as simple as detecting inherent marital problems (with the buyers only finding out later that the house was a divorce sale), substance abuse, financial difficulties, or health issues.

Layout of a house can divulge a great deal. A house with aligned front and back doors (the proverbial 'shotgun shack') has problems with air circulation and privacy (see Figure 9.4). Bedrooms at the end of long hallways give sleeping occupants the creepy feeling that something is running down the hall towards them. Areas suffering from a lack of sunlight cause occupants to feel depressed (and oppressed). Improper orientation makes a house stifling hot in summer and carry a perpetual Antarctic chill in winter.

A feng-shui practitioner can also detect any number of issues that an inspection might uncover. I have had clients more than once marvel that I knew where all the electrical, telephone, and cable outlets were even before they did. Other things I find might not

Figure 9.4

Frank Lloyd Wright's version of a shotgun shack: the Ennis House (built 1923) in southern California. From a model in DesignWorkshop Lite.

occur to them even after months of occupation. Simple observations of site slope can uncover potential pools of standing water. The feng-shui principle of 'smelling' can detect the aroma of fungus or mould. Add to these mundane abilities the ability to calculate the qualitative potential of a structure and feng shui becomes a fascinating diagnostic tool.

Chapter 10

An overview of the theory of time and space

*B*asic time calculations used in feng shui reflect calendar systems based on Chinese astronomy. Just as the Hetu is a map through the universe and it emerged from the Milky Way (the *Tian Ho* or celestial Yellow River), the Luoshu emerged from a tributary of the Milky Way, possibly near the Great Rift in the Western constellation of Cygnus (consisting of some of the Chinese constellation *Tianjin*, 'ford in the Celestial River').[1] At that spot in the sky we can see between two of our galaxy's spiral arms; the opening continues to Sagittarius (near the Chinese constellation of *Bie*, the turtle). Supposedly, the Luoshu's nine numbers were seen or scribbled on the back of a tortoise or bear, but they were eventually mapped onto China as part of the nonary grid system known as 'well-field' or *fenye*.

The Chinese lunisolar calendar appears on turtle shells known as 'oracle bones' dated to the period of Shang (fourteenth-century BCE). Shang-era astronomers calculated the 19-year *zhang* (Westerners call it the Metonic cycle, after Meton who lived in the fifth-century BCE) and the 76-year *bu* (what Westerners call the Calippic cycle, after another Greek astronomer active during the fourth-century BCE). According to astronomical records from oracle bones the civil year began at a new moon near the winter solstice. The *shang yuan* (superior epoch) or *taiji shang yuan* (supreme pole superior epoch) began at midnight on the first day of the 11th month, according to the *Daming li* (great brilliance calendar). This calculation was based on the time needed to align the synodic month with the tropical year.

In June 1993, astronomers Kevin Pang of JPL and John Bangert of the Naval Observatory revealed the start cycle of the Chinese calendar as 5 March 1953 BCE, when the sun, moon, Mercury, Venus, Mars, Jupiter, and Saturn queued 'like a pearl necklace' in the eastern sky just before dawn, next to what Westerners call the Pegasus Square. This occasion marked the *jiazi* or 'initial year' of the calendar cycle, just as the *jiazi* of the current cycle began on 2 February 1984.

Construction cycles

All buildings conform to construction cycles, which are defined as 20-year cycles based on calendar periods and work as initial conditions in complexity theory. The nine-sector grid of the Luoshu is used to plot these 'stars'. The number assigned to a particular 20-year cycle—sometimes called by names like 'ruling star'—is plotted at the centre of the diagram. (Often the term 'star' is used to indicate an element of a calculation. It is just feng-shui jargon for a particular integer in a formula.) Other calculations (such as orientation) are assigned numeric equivalents and plotted on the diagram, which provides the 'phase space' or event model of a structure. This grid enables a feng-shui practitioner to make qualitative and quantitative assessments using expert rules and the look-up tables that form every decent practitioner's bag of tricks.

Calculations involve 'three round (cycles) and nine fortune (types)'. Numbers 1 through 9 repeat 20 times to match three *ganzhi* (stem and branch) cycles of 180 years (known as *san yuan* or 'three epochs'). *Ji* and *yuan* in these calculations express units of calendrical calculations (*lifa*) that associate stem–branch combinations with astronomical periods. Explaining it another way, a *ganzhi* cycle consists of five orbits of Jupiter divided into three 20-year periods that each move through four of the 12 Jupiter stations (see Figure 10.1).

Yuan are found in the ancient *sifen li* (quarter-day) calendar,[2] but the 'three sequences' or *Santong li* calendar of Liu Xin is the current basis for construction cycle calculations.[3] The *Santong li* was a refinement of the *Taichu* calendar and consists of the following cycles.[4]

Rule cycle

The first day of the month of the civil calendar is the day of the new moon. *Zhang* identifies when the new moon returns to the same day in the solar year, usually the winter solstice. The unit of measure is the so-called Metonic cycle (235 lunations in 19 years).

Figure 10.1

Jupiter cycles form one of the important astronomical markers still found in feng shui. Photo credit: NASA.

Obscuration cycle

One *bu* = 4 *zhang* for a total of 76 years (the so-called Calippic cycle).

Epoch cycle

One *yuan* = 3 *ji*, 650 *bu*, or 240 *zhang* (4560 years).

Cycles are designated as high (water), middle (wood), and low (metal). They provide a layer of analysis that works with annual cycles and building orientations (see Table 10.1).

Each 20-year cycle encompasses psychological and historical events. The advent of the eight cycle, it is said, heralds a greater understanding of traditional feng shui in the west and increased emphasis on our need to integrate human structures and culture into the natural world.

Table 10.1

Construction cycles and basic analogy maps

20-Year cycle number	Gregorian date range	Five element designation
1	1864–1883	Water
2	1884–1903	Soil
3	1904–1923	Wood
4	1924–1943	Wood
5	1944–1963	Earth
6	1964–1983	Metal
7	1984–2003	Metal
8	2004–2023	Earth
9	2024–2044	Fire

Notes

[1] The Luo River is a tributary of the Yellow River in the sky and on Earth.

[2] The quarter-day calendar was in use by at least the fifth century BCE. It was replaced by the Taichu calender in 104 BCE.

[3] The *Santong li* was developed sometime around 26 BCE.

[4] See Cullen (1996, pp. 24–5).

Chapter 11

Form and shape theory in
time and space theory

*F*eng shui as a site selection theory provides the analytical techniques to assess structures of any time period. Like any systems science feng shui is contextual. A building is a chaotic system, in that it is characterized by extreme sensitivity to initial conditions. A minute change in an initial state can lead over time to large-scale consequences (including revenge effects). Ultimately, there are no parts at all—just a network of relationships. The way to understand and track the change is through calculations used in feng shui.

Without the aspect of time it is impossible to understand what happens. Subtle changes can give rise to self-reinforcing feedback loops. For example, the leafing and flowering of a tree can partially, albeit temporarily, remedy the incorrect siting of a reversed house.

Thomas Lee May[1] presents a case study of a Qing family town in Wu Xi approximately 100 km northwest of Shanghai. In the last nine cycles the town was very rich but eventually lost its great wealth due to the influence of *qi* from the eastern direction, which May tracks through time. May also makes a good case for the predictive modelling techniques of feng shui in his analysis of a fire at Southeast University, Nanjing. He shows how the 'fire possibility index' reached a peak around midnight on 12 December 1912, which was when the fire occurred. May thinks it likely that the predictive techniques available to a feng-shui practitioner could locate areas of concern for fires, personal safety, illness, and cultural and personality development.[2]

With these thoughts in mind let us consider some possible ramifications of building orientation and design. Particular orientations can build in problems ranging from fires, accidents, and calamities to the bizarre and anomalous. Figures 11.1 and 11.2 convey orientations in recent and future building cycles that can create such problems. Without adequate feng-shui advice a builder can expect a variety of troubles with these structures. Additional orientations can cause problems if not provided with supportive design and landscaping.

Figure 11.1

Orientations of questionable structures for the period 4 February 1984 to 4 February 2004

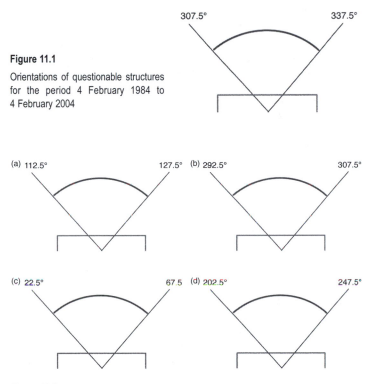

Figure 11.2

Orientations of questionable structures for the period 4 February 2004 to 4 February 2024.

Notes

[1] See May (1995).

[2] See May (1995).

Chapter 12

Services

*L*ayout of services in new homes follows building codes, but their placement and integration with room layout can improve with the addition of feng shui. For example, fireplaces, heating and air conditioning systems, computer clusters, and massive entertainment centres do best in areas where they do not trigger revenge effects—whether it is powerful magnetic fields or something more subtle, such as an amplifying feng-shui calculation (see Figure 12.1).

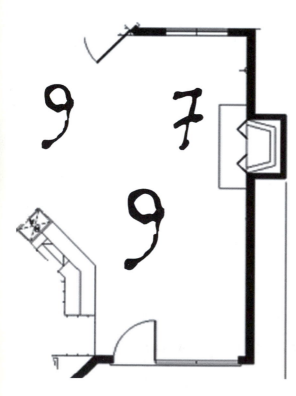

Figure 12.1

Placement of a fireplace to coincide with a 9 (the number of fire) can exacerbate revenge effects.

Electrical services

The issue is not the imaginary 'geopathic stress' or the number of outlets and fixtures in a room but whether ambient magnetic fields will clash with installed services. Thankfully, designs that reduce electrical consumption also reduce magnetic fields. Fields drop dramatically with distance (they are proportional to current flow), but it is still important to ensure the safety of occupants.

One way to check is with the feng-shui analysis—especially whether a room's intended function matches the placement of outlets. Remedies consist of hiding outlets and fixtures, swapping room functions, and similar avoidance techniques. Optimally, the solution is to design rooms according to the feng-shui analysis, which correlates function to placement (see Figure 12.2).

Figure 12.2

Room function that coincides with feng-shui analysis.

Feng shui often looks askance at the placement of bedrooms next to kitchens and baths for reasons invented long before the advent of indoor plumbing and power grids. However, if you plan to place a bedroom against the wall of a kitchen or another room with multiple appliances, ensure that exposure to magnetic fields will not cause problems—after all, magnetic fields do not stop at the wall unless it contains magnetic shielding (aluminum, low-carbon steel, silicon-iron steel, or mumetal). Use active magnetic field cancellation to substantially reduce field exposure. Do not let metal-sheathed (BX) cable rest on appliances, heating pipes, or grounded water pipes because current returns to the service panel or transformer through the ground and creates a magnetic field. Try installing dielectric couplers on plumbing lines to eliminate any possibility of currents.

Large magnetic fields are typically created in the power panels. Mount these boxes where exposure to fields will be minimal (such as a garage wall or on an outside closet wall). Run wires from a service panel several metres from areas in frequent use. If power is brought in overhead, try to avoid having it run down along bedroom walls or the walls of other heavily used rooms. A better solution is to run wires underneath the flooring and bring them up to outlets.

Effective shielding from electric fields requires grounded objects; otherwise, fields from transformers, microwave ovens, older computer monitors, electrical lines and conduit, and electrical panels are unlikely to be stopped. That is why effective design places kitchen appliances away from bedroom and living room walls, or any place where people spend considerable time. Similarly, place ground-floor fluorescent ceiling fixtures away from second-floor areas of high use at floor level.

It is the same issue with any 'phantom load', such as televisions and microwaves that consume electricity even when switched off. Use switched outlets for entertainment centres and other phantom loads to reduce magnetic fields.

Avoid radiant heating systems that generate fields above 2 mG at less than a meter. Draft exposure guidelines set by the

International Radiation Protection Association provide 5 kV/m for continuous exposure to electric fields and 2 G for magnetic fields.

Water service

The developed world frequently forgets that not everyone has easy access to potable water. In Mexico City, for example, more than three million people lack indoor plumbing. Even those people who are linked to the city's system have to endure its antiquated and inadequate service. This scenario is repeated throughout the world. According to the United Nations Population Fund in their *State of the World Population 2001*, unclean water and associated poor sanitation kill more than 12 million people each year. The World Health Organization reports that roughly 1.1 billion people do not have any access to clean water. In developing countries, more than 90 per cent of sewage and 70 per cent of industrial wastes are dumped, untreated, into surface waters.

Covering drains for fear of losing money—an adage common to some flavours of feng-shui books—is at best a neurotic conceit when compared with the water stress elsewhere on the planet.[1] Without addressing everyone's need for potable water there is no point in tackling what amount to lifestyle issues in the developed world.

Perhaps the simplest advice is this: do not install pipes in walls adjacent to bedrooms without adequate insulation against noise. No one enjoys listening to gurgling pipes.

Note

[1] A human receiving less than 1000 cubic meters of water each year falls under the scientific ceiling that signals 'water stress'. In the Middle East, nine of 14 countries currently experience water scarcity. California, northern China, the Sahel, and southern Europe will experience it in the near future (Samson and Charrier, 1997).

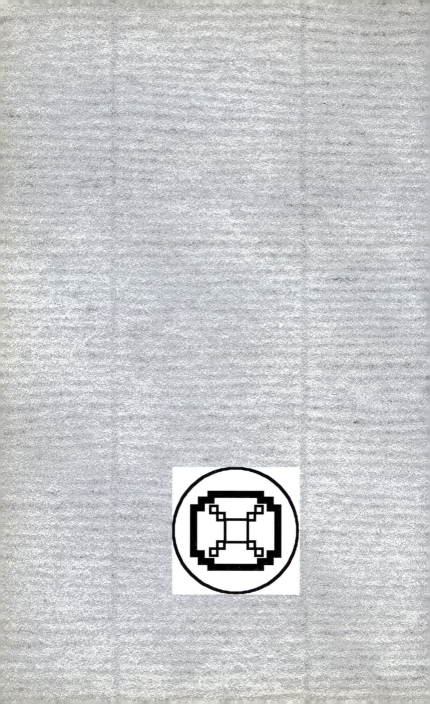

Chapter 13

Overlooked and overblown issues of
drainage, water supply and storage,
ventilation, electrical supply and
installation, lighting, and sound

Drainage

Drainage carries an undeserved reputation in most feng-shui books. People are made to worry needlessly about stopping their drains and faucets when they need to concentrate on ecology and environmental justice.

Drainage issues are comparatively simple—revenge effects occur because drainage is misunderstood. Drainage develops where types and structures of rock erode easily and their ability to drain relates to topography, soil type, bedrock type, climate, and vegetation. It has nothing to do with 'energy lines', 'dragon lines', or any other animal trails—or much else that people are encouraged to believe. The truly sinister stuff comes from the handiwork of humans (see Figure 13.1).

Wetlands are regularly drained to turn land into subdivisions, commercial buildings, and industrial parks, which create such revenge effects as environmental degradation, reduced (and often irremediable) water quality, increased pollution, loss of ecological

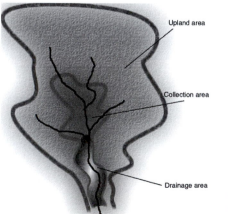

Upland area

Collection area

Drainage area

Figure 13.1

Drainage identified as a feng-shui issue.

sustainability, soil erosion and sedimentation, and the aesthetic loss of natural beauty. Artificial drainage systems are rarely designed with the whole picture in mind. That is why they generally fail to capitalize on the wider ecological and aesthetic role of water.

So much for the so-called advancements in modern civilization! Natural or undeveloped areas reap the advantage of natural processes that recycle material—including pollutants—running off the land during rainstorms. Surface runoff in developed areas cannot use the natural world in the same way.

Consider implementing the following suggestions:

- reduce the effect of development on natural drainage;
- protect and enhance water quality;
- cherish and respect the environmental setting by obtaining intimate knowledge of a place and the biophilic needs of the local community, and incorporate them into the design;
- provide wildlife habitat;
- encourage natural groundwater recharge.

Water supply and storage

One of the oldest Chinese characters is 'well' and it is apparently related to feng shui through the well-field system of land holding. One of the well-field's most ancient forms is a 3×3 square grid like the Luoshu.[1] However, this ancient connection has not stopped the McFengshui crowd from inventing odd ideas about wells, ponds, swimming pools, and spas.

Thankfully, traditional feng shui is not as neurotic as the New Age variety. With traditional feng shui you have adequate tools to effectively plan a site for large amounts of water and it is also possible to remedy existing sites. There should be no need to resort to overwrought symbolism or other refuges of the ill-informed, who often get their ideas from Hollywood (*Poltergeist* and *The Amityville Horror*, for example) or old occult literature.

Ventilation

Traditional cultures orient their homes to take advantage of prevailing winds, an idea that should be reinforced in modern architecture. Similarly, windows have to be used to be effective; there should not be any hand-wringing over 'energy' leaking out or in from closed windows, unless the seal is not tight. Often what McFengshui practitioners call 'energy' is not solar gain, moisture, or any number of identifiable elements—it is what practitioners say when they need a technical-sounding term. So how this vague 'energy' substance could be draining from a house or entering through a closed window is beyond all comprehension.

It is best to ignore these would-be pundits when they talk about 'energy' drains or gains through windows. Instead, look at what is done with ventilation in traditional architecture, and copy that. At least then you are dealing with concepts that are proven to work.

Electrical supply and installation

As explained in Chapter 12, plenty of real-world issues exist regarding electricity in a structure so there is need for inventing things like 'geopathic stress' or the hobgoblins of baubiology. However, the real issues have not stopped some practitioners from making up 'energy fields' that cannot be measured or treated except by the most bizarre methods—such as dowsing, psychic vibrations, and misguided applications of voltmeters.

Keep in mind that most feng-shui practitioners do not have a solid science education and thus are prone to get things of that nature completely wrong. Remain sceptical and make a practitioner prove any wacky theories beyond a reasonable doubt. And even then, check with a science-savvy friend.

Lighting

This subject is dear to the McFengshui crowd but like so many other things they generally get it wrong. Whether it is their bizarre

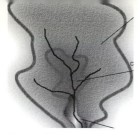

notions of light therapy (unfortunately, not along the lines of proven methods to cure Seasonal Affective Disorder) or how to illuminate sections of a structure, they fail to take into account basic human physiology and psychology.

A practitioner suggests high-powered illumination on the porch outside a home to 'bring in *qi*' or whatever they hope to draw. However, if there are steps, a bright light on a porch can create accidents because people tend to focus on the distraction and not where their feet are going—so they miss the step, slip, and fall. That is probably not the sort of *qi* that the occupant was hoping to attract.

Others want you to place lights at angles around a structure to give the effect that any so-called missing areas exist. Why portions of a structure should be deemed 'missing' is a mystery, as is how floodlights would remedy this. It seems to be a technique that runs on the placebo effect.

Sometimes practitioners want people to place a hollow tube in the ground and add a light bulb on the top, ostensibly to draw *qi* out of the ground. Perhaps this technique is supposed to work like my grandfather's technique for catching worms before we went fishing, only he used a bit of current on a wire running to a wire coat hanger and stuck that into the ground to attract the worms. Unfortunately, for people who get sucked into using this *qi*-siphon method, there is no way to measure its effectiveness, unlike my grandfather's worm lure.

Sound

I have neighbours I have nicknamed the Loud Family. Everyone encounters people like this sometime in their life. You can choose to ignore them or try any number of things to discourage their vocal abilities. The McFengshui crowd wants you to use mirrors.

The favoured New Age technique for noisy neighbours beneath you in a flat is to place a mirror face-down on the floor. Of course there is no way to measure its effectiveness; and, strangely, this is the 'cure' of choice rather than having a chat with the offending party regarding their noise level. There are any number of feng-shui books on the market that tell people to use mirrors to deflect noise—then they crow about the practicality of feng shui.

Obviously, something out of the realm of soundproofing or asking a noisy neighbour to be quiet is too mundane for some feng-shui practitioners, but these prosaic techniques do provide more lasting relief.

Note

[1] See Berglund (1990, pp. 69–70).

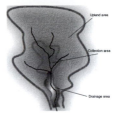

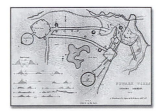

Chapter 14

Building elements

Enhancing placement of stairs and gradients, fireplaces, doors, and windows

Stairs and gradients

You might not like living in a shotgun shack, but what could be worse than living in a house where the interior staircase ends on a line with the front door? Call it bad feng shui or accident-prone, it is all the same. In fact, many alleged feng-shui problems on further examination turn out to be design problems.

Humans, especially children and the visually impaired, need as few distractions as possible to safely navigate a flight of stairs. In legal terms, stairs are an 'attractive nuisance' that create risk because architects and builders typically locate stairs where they are the most dangerous (see Figure 14.1).[1] Considering that the top and bottom two steps are where the majority of accidents on stairs occur,[2] it makes perfect sense not to align stairs with doors or have doors on a landing open onto a flight of stairs (see Figure 14.2).

Some feng-shui practitioners say that an interior staircase exiting to an exterior door compels money and good things to leave the premises. There is abundant anecdotal evidence, but to my

Figure 14.1

Bad feng shui or bad design? The stairs aligned with front door makes arguments for either label. From a model in DesignWorkshop Lite.

Figure 14.2

A common stair design that is one of the most accident prone. This version is at Fallingwater. From a model in DesignWorkshop Lite.

knowledge no practitioner can provide adequate documentation to substantiate this claim.

Some practitioners claim that a particular number of steps can create problems and accidents, but the facts argue otherwise.[3] However, it is known that a stairway designed to induce changes in orientation—such as view, lighting, route direction, level, etc.—is a higher risk for accidents because of the level of distraction designed into it. Additionally, complex stair layouts (including helical and dogleg) should be designed so that people do not need to make abrupt turns and ascend clockwise to ease traffic flow (see Figure 14.3).[4]

A popular McFengshui tactic is to suggest a bright light for a dimly lit area outside a front door. This seems sensible until you review accident statistics. A bright light at a front door with steps actually creates more accidents than it prevents—if indeed this technique has that effect—because the intensity of the light makes it more difficult to see the stair. Poorly lit steps are just as dangerous as brightly lit ones. A lighting solution that makes it impossible to miss the step is the best answer (see Figure 14.4).

Figure 14.3

Complex stair layouts create navigation problems. This stair is in the Larkin Building. From a model in DesignWorkshop Lite.

(a)

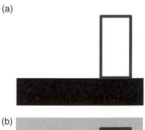

(b)

Figure 14.4

The bright light at a front door creates as many accidents as dim lighting.

Windows and artificial light sources placed near stairs are also problems. Some practitioners worry about the effect of 'energy' coming through the window or from a light source, but accident researchers argue that the real risk results from someone having to include these objects *and* the stairs in their field of vision.[5]

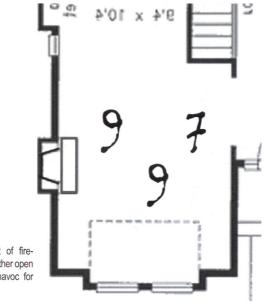

Figure 14.5
Improper placement of fireplaces, stoves, and other open flames can create havoc for occupants.

Fireplaces

There is nothing cozier than a crackling, warm fire on a wintry evening. But what if the fireplace has been oriented so that it figuratively 'burns up' someone's health, career, and/or relationships? In a subdivision it is possible that several floorplans provide just this type of distress. Mitigating these effects requires knowledge of advanced feng shui practices and calculations (see Figure 14.5).

Doors

The advice given for stairs applies to doors as well. Lining up doorways may be aesthetically pleasing to some but it does create risk for accidents. A feng-shui practitioner might express theories about this kind of situation that range from the innocuous (possible friction and arguments between people who occupy two bedrooms in this kind of configuration) to the insane (overwrought symbolism in one form or another).

Moreover, according to *ba zhai*, the orientation and positioning of doorways provide insights into health, wealth, and relationship

issues. Sometimes doorways have to be changed or avoided to alleviate problems for occupants. Such changes are best made on a case-by-case basis.

Windows

Just because someone worries about 'energy' coming in or leaking out of a window does not mean there is a problem. The issue of windows is generally overblown unless the window looks out onto an ugly or demoralizing viewshed. Why some practitioners worry at length about windows and ignore their history in Asian architecture is beyond the scope of this book.

Materials

Comments on various materials to correct problems with existing structures and to avoid problems

Small is good

Building size should not be dictated by image, it should reflect function. In the last three decades, the average floor area of an American house has increased 77 per cent as households have shrunk. (Some feng-shui practitioners link the construction cycle number to the household size—with metal years notorious for creating family dysfunction and divorce.) Not only is this increase in floor area wasteful, when people step outside their McMansions they are confronted with a degraded environment caused by this unwarranted expansion in personal space (see Figure 14.6).

Be effective in resource management

In many cases, the greatest harm to the natural environment (and the greatest expenses to people, businesses, and governing bodies) results from building on undeveloped land. Seek out sites in already developed areas; consider rehabilitating or remodelling an existing structure.

Figure 14.6

Thanks to sprawl and the ubiquitous McMansion there's sprawl and environmental degradation like this. Photo by the author.

Stick with simple
People waste money and materials on gratuitous complexity and decorations instead of creating timeless structures that appeal to a sense of craftsmanship and elegant design.

Eschew rigid designs
Structures that allow a variety of functions require less remodelling than structures built for a fleeting niche market.

Build for remodelling
Reducing valuable materials to rubble with a bulldozer or wrecking ball is not efficient or environment-friendly. Design in the use of bolts, screws, and recyclable composites.

Look to the future
Design and build for generations to come. Carefully crafted structures stand the test of time and cost less.

Notes

1 See Templer (1994, pp. 113, 136–7, 140–1).
2 See Templer (1994, p. 113).
3 See Templer (1994, p. 140).
4 See Templer (1994, p. 139).
5 See Templer (1994, pp. 145–6).

Chapter 15

Resources

Feng-shui books for further reading

Books by Lam Kam Chuen, Raymond Lo, Larry Sang, Eva Wong; and by Elizabeth Moran, Joseph Yu, and Val Biktashev (March 8, 2002). 'Complete Idiot's Guide to Feng Shui', Alpha Books, 2nd edition.

Feng-shui instruction and information

American Feng Shui Institute, http://www.amfengshui.com/

Feng Shui and Destiny with Raymond Lo, http://www.raymond-lo.com/

Feng Shui Research Center (Joseph Yu), http://www.astro-fengshui.com/

Feng Shui Ultimate Resource, http://www.qi-whiz.com/

Feng-Shui information (Eva Wong), http://www.shambhala.com/fengshui/

Yap Cheng Hai Centre of Excellence, http://www.ychfengshui.com/

Green building and other sustainable technologies

Architectural Acoustics Consulting, Noise Control, http://www.orpheus-acoustics.com/home.html

Arctic Circle: Social Equity and Environmental Justice, http://arcticcircle.uconn.edu/SEEJ/

Backyard Habitat Program of the National Wildlife Federation, http://www.nwf.org/backyardwildlifehabitat/

Cal Earth Forum, http://www.calearth.org/

Center of Excellence for Sustainable Development, http://www.sustainable.doe.gov/

Congress for the New Urbanism, http://www.cnu.org/

Cyburbia, http://www.cyburbia.org/

EcoIQ Home: Sustainable Communties, Businesses, & Households, http://www.ecoiq.com/

EcoJustice Network, http://www.igc.org/envjustice/

EcoTimber, http://www.ecotimber.com/info/specification.asp

EnviroNet Base, http://www.environetbase.com/home.asp

Environmental Building News, http://www.buildinggreen.com

Environmental Design and Construction, http://www.edcmag.com/CDA/BNPHomePage/1,4111,,00.html

Environmental Justice Resource, http://www.ejrc.cau.edu/

Factor Four, http://www.bsdglobal.com/tools/principles_factor.asp

Global Issues, http://www.globalissues.org/

Green Roofs for Healthy Cities, http://www.peck.ca/grhcc/main.htm

Honor the Earth, http://www.honorearth.com/

Humane Street Lighting, http://www.uvm.edu/histpres/HPJ/streetlights/index.html

Implosion, http://home.worldcom.ch/~negenter/

Indigenous Environmental Network, http://www.ienearth.org/

Katarxis, http://luciensteil.tripod.com/katarxis/index.html

James Howard Kunstler, http://www.kunstler.com/

PatternLanguage, http://www.patternlanguage.com/

PLANETIZEN: Planning & Development News, Jobs, & Events, http://www.planetizen.com/

Planum—European Journal of Planning Online, http://www. planum.net/

Population Reference Bureau, http://www.prb.org/

Resurrecting Classical Land Use Patterns, http://www.villageat.org/

Skillful Means, Design and Construction, Strawbale, http://www.skillful-means.com/index.html

Smart Architecture, http://www.smartarch.nl/

Sprawl Watch, http://www.sprawlwatch.org/

Sustainable Architecture, Sustainable Development, http://www.sustainableabc.com/index.html

Traffic Calming—Your Complete Guide, http://www.trafficcalming.org/
Whole Building Design Guide, http://www.wbdg.org/index.asp

Space weather
Space Environment Center, http://sec.noaa.gov/

Bibliography

Adachi, Y., M. Shigomawara, M. Higuchi, Y. Haruta, and M. Ochiai (2000). Measurement of low frequency biomagnetic signals under non-periodical extramural noise by continuously adjusted least squares method. *Proceedings of the 12th International Conference on Biomagnetism*, pp. 899–902.

Ahern, Emily M. (1973). *The Cult of the Dead in a Chinese Village*. Stanford.

Alexander, Christopher (1977). *A Pattern Language*. Oxford University Press.

Alexander, Christopher (1979). *The Timeless Way of Building*. Oxford University Press.

Allan, Sarah (1991). *The Shape of the Turtle: Myth, Art, and Cosmos in Early China*. SUNY Press.

American Academy of Microbiology (1–3 December 2000). *Geobiology: Exploring the Interface Between the Biosphere and the Geosphere*.

An, Zhimin, translated by W. Tsao (1991). On the origin of Chinese civilization. *Journal of Henan Normal University* **18** (3), 67–72.

Anton, Mike, and Henry Chu (2002). Welcome to Orange County, California. *Los Angeles Times Valley Edition*, 9 March 2002, front page.

Arie, Peled, and Schwartz Hava (March 1999). Exploring the ideal home in psychotherapy: two case studies. *Journal of Environmental Psychology* **19** (1), 87–94.

Ascher, Marcia (2002). *Mathematics Elsewhere: An Exploration of Ideas Across Cultures*. Princeton University Press.

Athanasiou, Tom (1998). *Divided Planet: The Ecology of Rich and Poor*. University of Georgia Press.

Atlas, Randall (March 2001). The other side of CPTED. *Security Management Magazine*.

August, Oliver, and Norman Hammond (31 October 2002). Chinese dig up relics from 'majestic' town of 6000 BC. *Times Online* (http://www.timesonline.co.uk).

Bach-y-Rita, Paul, Kurt A. Kaczmarek, Mitchell E. Tyler, Jorge Garcia-Lara (October 1998). Form perception with a 49-point electrotactile stimulus array on the tongue: a technical note. *Journal of Rehabilitation Research and Development* **35** (4), 427–30.

Ball, Philip (20 August 2002). Urban sprawl creates unwilling neighbours. *Nature Science Update* (http://www.nature.com/nsu/020819/ 0208191.html).

Ballentine, Chris J., Peter E. van Keken, Don Porcelli, and Erik H. Hauri (15 November 2002). Numerical models, geochemistry and the zero-paradox noble-gas mantle. *Philosophical Transactions: Mathematical, Physical and Engineering Sciences. Proceedings of the Royal Society, Series A* **360** (1800). DOI: 10.1098/rsta.2002.1083.

Bamford, Christopher (ed.) (1994). *Rediscovering Sacred Science*. Floris.

Bender, Kenneth J. (July 2000). Transcranial magnetic stimulation reduces auditory hallucinations. *Psychiatric Times* **XVII** (7).

Berglund, Lars (1990). *The Secret of Luo Shu: Numerology in Chinese Art and Architecture*. Södra Sandby.

Berman, Morris (2000). *Wandering God: A Study in Nomadic Spirituality*. SUNY Press.

Bonham Jr., J. Blaine, Gerri Spilka, and Darl Rastorfer (2002). *Old Cities, Green Cities: Communities Transform Unmanaged Land*. APA Advisory Service.

Boyd, Andrew (1962). *Chinese Architecture and Town Planning 1500 BC–AD 1911*. Alec Tirani.

Brand, Stewart (1995). *How Buildings Learn: What Happens After They're Built*. Penguin.

Brecher, Kenneth, and Michael Feirtag (1981). *Astronomy of the Ancients*. MIT Press.

Brennan, Martin (1983). *The Stars and the Stones: Ancient Art and Astronomy in Ireland*. Thames and Hudson.

Brown, David E., Mindy Fox, and Mary Rickel Pelletier (eds) (2000). *Sustainable Architecture White Papers*. Earth Pledge Foundation.

Brown, M. Gordon (1998). *Design and Value: Spatial Form and the Economic Failure of a Mall*. Space Analytics, LLC. Presented at the 14th Annual Meeting of the American Real Estate Society.

Brown, M. Gordon (21 May 1999). 'Are we closing ourselves out?' Viewpoint. *Denver Business Journal*.

Brown, M. Gordon (2001). *Healthy Sidewalks: A Guide*. Space Analytics, LLC.

Bullard, Robert D. (ed.) (1993). *Confronting Environmental Racism: Voices from the Grassroots*. South End Press.

Burden, Dan, and Peter Lagerwey (1999). *Road Diets: Fixing the Big Roads*. Walkable Communities, Inc.

Burger, J. (2002). Restoration, stewardship, environmental health, and policy: understanding stakeholders' perceptions. *Environmental Management* **30** (5), 631–40.

Campbell, Wallace H. (1997). *Introduction to Geomagnetic Fields*. Cambridge.

Cao Bingwu (translator) (24 December 2000). News from Lingjiatan, a famous prehistoric site in Anhui Province. *China Cultural Relics News*.

Capra, Fritjof (1996). *The Web of Life*. Anchor Doubleday.

Chang, K.C. (1976). *Early Chinese Civilization: Anthropological Perspectives*. Harvard University Press.

Chang, K.C. (1983). *Art, Myth and Ritual: The Path to Political Authority in Ancient China*. Harvard University Press.

Cheng Jian Jun, and Adriana Fernandes-Gonçalves (1998). *Chinese Feng Shui Compass: Step by Step Guide*. Jiangxi Sciences and Technology.

Chou Yeu-Ming (1999). *The Urban Planning of Chinese Ancient Cities*. 1stBooks.

Clay, Grady (1973). *Close-Up: How to View the American City*. Praeger.

Cohn, Norman (2001). *Warrant for Genocide*. Serif.

Coley, R.L., F.E. Kuo, and W.C. Sullivan (1997). Where does community grow? The social context created by nature in urban public housing. *Environment & Behaviour* **29** (4), 468–92.

Coleman, Daniel A. (1994). *Ecopolitics: Building a Green Society*. Rutgers University Press.

Cowley et al. (15 November 2002). Solar–wind–magnetosphere–ionosphere interactions in the Earth's plasma environment. *Philosophical Transactions: Mathematical, Physical and Engineering Sciences. Proceedings of the Royal Society, Series A* **360** (1800). DOI: 10.1098/rsta.2002.1112.

Cox, John J., David S. Maehr, and Jeffery L. Larkin (August 2002). The biogeography of faunal place names in the United States. *Conservation Biology* **16** (4), 1143–50.

Craven, Rebecca (2002). Attention to detail. *Nature Reviews Neuroscience* **3**, 764. DOI: 10.1038/nrh953.

Crowe, Norman (1995). *Nature and the Idea of a Man-Made World*. MIT Press.

Cullen, Christopher (1996). *Astronomy and Mathematics in Ancient China: The Zhou Bi Suan Jing*. Cambridge University Press.

De Araujo, D.B., O. Baffa, and R.T. Wakai (2000). Theta and alpha oscillations: dependency on navigation tasks. *Proceedings of the 12th International Conference on Biomagnetism*, pp. 343–6.

Deasy, C.M. (1985). *Designing Places for People*. Whitney Library of Design.

DeAmicis, Ralph and Lahni (2001). *Feng Shui and the Tango in Twelve Easy Lessons: Why Feng Shui Works and How to Make it Work for You*. Cuore Libre.

Delfino, Ralph J. et al. (1997). Effects of air pollution on emergency room visits for respiratory illnesses in Montreal, Quebec. *American Journal of Respiratory and Critical Care Medicine* **155**, 568–76.

Devereaux, Paul (1994). *Shamanism and the Mystery Lines: Ley Lines, Spirit Paths, Shape-Shifting and Out-of-Body Travel*. Llewellyn.

DeWoskin, Kenneth J. (1983). *Doctors, Diviners, and Magicians of Ancient China: Biographies of Fang-shih*. Columbia University Press.

Dong, Li-zhang (2002). The races descended from the deities who regarded the Azure Dragon, the Vermilion Bird and the White Tiger as their Totems and the Great Ancient Tomb in Xishuipo, Puyang. *Journal of Sun Yatsen University, Social Science Edition* **42** (2).

Duany, Andres, Elizabeth Plater-Zyberk, and Jeff Speck (2000). *Suburban Nation: The Rise of Sprawl and the Decline of the American Dream*. North Point Press.

Dunne, Jennifer A., Richard J. Williams, and Neo D. Martinez (2002). Food-web structure and network theory: the role of connectance and size. *Proceedings of the National Academy Sciences of the USA*, **99** (20), 12917–22.

Dye, Lee (16 May 2002). *Blinded by the Light: Data Shows Night Lighting in Buildings Kills Birds* (http://www.abcnews.com).

Edge, Frank (2000–2001). Aurochs in the sky. A celestial interpretation of the Hall of Bulls in the Cave of Lascaux. *Paper Presented at INSAP III*.

Egretta Sutton, Sharon, and Susan P. Kemp (March 2002). Children as partners in neighborhood placemaking: lessons from intergenerational design charrettes. *Journal of Environmental Psychology*, **22** (1/2), 171–89.

Eliade, Mircea (1991). *The Myth of the Eternal Return; Or, Cosmos and History*, 9th edn. Princeton University Press.

Evans, Gary, Peter Lercher, and Walter F. Kofler (September 2002). Crowding and children's mental health: the role of house type. *Journal of Environmental Psychology* **22** (3), 221–31.

Evans, Gary W., and Janetta Mitchell McCoy (March 1998). When buildings don't work: the role of architecture in human health. *Journal of Environmental Psychology* **18** (1), 85–94.

Executive Department, Maine State Planning Office (1997). *The Cost of Sprawl*.

Faber Taylor, Andrea, Frances Kuo, and William C. Sullivan (March 2002). Views of nature and self-discipline: evidence from inner city children. *Journal of Environmental Psychology* **22** (1/2), 49–63.

Fagan, William F., Eli Meir, Steven S. Carroll, and Jianguo Wu (January 2001). The ecology of urban landscapes: modeling housing starts as a density-dependent colonization process. *Landscape Ecology* **16** (1), 33–9.

Fang, Zitao (2000). *Feng shui in site planning and design: a new perspective for sustainable development*. Master's thesis, Arizona State University.

Gajendran, Jyothiram (2000). *Playing upon patient psychology in hospital environment*. Indian Express Group (http://www.expresshealth-caremgmt.com).

Gardiner, Martin (1957). *Fads and Fallacies in the Name of Science*. Dover.

Gardiner, Martin (1978). *The Ambidextrous Universe: Mirror Asymmetry and Time-Reversed Worlds*. Scribner.

Gedicks, A.L. (1993). *The New Resource Wars: Native and Environmental Struggles Against Multinational Corporations*. South End Press.

Gentz, Joachim (1998). The system of the 'monthly ordinances' (yueling). *Paper presented at the Eighth International Conference on the History of Science in China*.

Geo Factsheet (1998). *Urban Microclimates*, vol. 50, September.

George, Mark S., Sarah H. Lisanby, and Harold A. Sackeim (1999). Transcranial magnetic stimulation: applications in neuropsychiatry. *Archives of General Psychiatry* **56**, 300–11.

Gobet, J.M. (1998). *Geobiology—The Holistic House.* Transformation Network (http://www.transformation.net/coils/geobiology.html).

Goldman, Michael (ed.) (1998). *Privatizing Nature: Political Struggles for the Global Commons.* Rutgers.

Goodrick-Clarke, Nicholos (1992). *The Occult Roots of Nazism: Secret Aryan Cults and their Influence on Nazi Ideology.* New York University Press.

Grossman, Wendy M. (15 May 2002). The shifting ground beneath your feet—new approaches to understanding the Earth's mantle. *A Summary of Chemical Reservoirs and Convection in the Earth's Mantle.* Royal Society.

Haeuber, Richard (July 1999). Sprawl tales: Maryland's smart growth initiative and the evolution of growth management. *Urban Ecosystems* **3** (2), 131–47.

Hallett, Mark (13 July 2000). Transcranial magnetic stimulation and the human brain. *Nature* **406**, 147–50.

Hamilton, W.D., and T.M. Lenton (March 1998). Spora and Gaia: how microbes fly with their clouds. *Ethology, Ecology and Evolution* **10**, 1–16.

Ham-Rowbottom, Kathleen A., Robert Gifford, and Kelly T. Shaw (June 1999). Defensible space theory and the police: assessing the vulnerability of residences to burglary. *Journal of Environmental Psychology* **19** (2), 117–29.

Hawken, Paul, Amory Lovins, and L. Hunter Lovins (1999). *Natural Capitalism: Creating the Next Industrial Revolution.* Little, Brown.

Heal, R.D., and A.T. Parsons (2002). Novel intercellular communication system in *Escherichia coli* that confers antibiotic resistance between physically separated populations. *Journal of Applied Microbiology* **92**, 1116–22.

Heath, Robin (1999). *Sun, Moon, and Earth.* Walker and Company.

Heerwagen, Judith H., and Gorden H. Orians (1993). 'Humans, Habitats, and Aesthetics'. In: Kellert, Stephen R. and Edward O. Wilson (eds). *The Biophilia Hypothesis.* Shearwater.

Herdeg, Klaus (1990). *Formal Structure in Indian Architecture.* Rizzoli.

Herzog, Thomas R., Hong C. Chen, and Jessica S. Primeau (September 2002). Perception of the restorative potential of natural and other settings. *Journal of Environmental Psychology* **22** (3), 295–306.

Hiss, Tony (1990). *The Experience of Place.* Knopf.

Ho Peng Yoke (2000). *Li, Qi and Shu: An Introduction to Science and Civilization in China*. Dover.

Hobbs, Richard J (December 2001). Synergisms among habitat fragmentation, livestock grazing, and biotic invasions in southwestern Australia. *Conservation Biology* **15** (6), 1522.

Hobbs, R.J., and J.A. Harris (June 2001). Restoration ecology: repairing the earth's ecosystems in the new millennium. *Restoration Ecology* **9** (2), 239–46.

Hoffman, Ralph E., Nashaat N. Boutros, Sylvia Hu, Robert M. Berman, John H. Krystal, and Dennis S. Charney (25th March 2000). Transcranial magnetic stimulation and auditory hallucinations in schizophrenia. *The Lancet* **355**, 1073–5.

Horelli, Liisa, and Mirkka Kaaja (2002). Opportunities and constraints of 'internet-assisted urban planning' with young people. *Journal of Environmental Psychology* **22** (1/2), 191–200.

Huang, Alfred (2000). *The Numerology of the I Ching*. Inner Traditions International.

Huston, Peter (1997). *Scams from the Great Beyond: How to Make Easy Money Off of ESP, Astrology, UFOs, Crop Circles, Cattle Mutilations, Alien Abductions, Atlantis, Channeling, and Other New Age Nonsense*. Paladin Press.

Hygge, Staffan, and Igor Knez (September 2001). Effects of noise, heat and indoor lighting on cognitive performance and self-reported affect. *Journal of Environmental Psychology* **21** (3), 291–9.

International Council for Science (2002a). *ICSU Series on Science for Sustainable Development No. 4: Science, Traditional Knowledge and Sustainable Development*.

International Council for Science (2002b). *Science and Traditional Knowledge: Report from the ICSU Study Group on Science and Traditional Knowledge*. Revised 23 June 2002.

Institute for East Asian Studies (1983–1985). *Early China*. Volumes 9–10. University of California at Berkeley.

Institute for East Asian Studies (1990). *Early China*. Volume 15. University of California at Berkeley.

Institute for East Asian Studies (1995). *Early China*. Volume 20. University of California at Berkeley.

Institute for East Asian Studies (1996). *Early China.* Volume 21. University of California at Berkeley.

Institute for East Asian Studies (1998–1999). *Early China.* Volumes 23–24. University of California at Berkeley.

Iverson, Louis R., and Elizabeth A. Cook (April 2000). Urban forest cover of the Chicago region and its relation to household density and income. *Urban Ecosystems* **4** (2), 105–24.

Jacobs, Jane (1992). *The Death and Life of Great American Cities.* Vintage.

James, Peter, and Nick Thrope (1999). *Ancient Mysteries.* Thames & Hudson.

Jarvilehto, Timo (1995). The theory of the organism-environment system: III. Role of efferent influences on receptors in the formation of knowledge. *Integrative Physiological and Behavioral Science* **34**, 90–100.

Jauch, J.M. (1973). *Are Quanta Real?* Indiana University Press.

Johnsson, Eric (2002). *Inner Navigation: Why We Get Lost and How We Find Our Way.* Scribner.

Jorgensen, Bradley S., and Richard C. Stedman (September 2001). Sense of place as an attitude: lakeshore owners attitudes toward their properties. *Journal of Environmental Psychology* **21** (3), 233–48.

Joseph, George Gheverghese (1991). *The Crest of the Peacock: Non-European Roots of Mathematics.* Penguin.

Kawakami, O., Y. Kaneoke, and R. Kakigi (2000). Perception of apparent motion is related to the magnetic response from the human extrastriate cortex. *Proceedings of the 12th International Conference on Biomagnetism*, pp. 161–4.

Keightley, David N. (1995). A measure of man in early China: in search of the neolithic inch. *Chinese Science* **12**, 18–40.

Kellert, Stephen R., and Edward O. Wilson (1993). *The Biophilia Hypothesis.* Shearwater.

Kellert, Stephen R. (1996). *The Value of Life: Biological Diversity and Human Society.* Shearwater.

Kirby, Alex (2002). *Progress 'undermines African cultures'.* BBC News, 8 May (http://news.bbc.co.uk/hi/english/sci/tech/newsid_1975000/ 1975359.stm).

Knoll, Max. (1983). Transformations of science in our age. In Joseph Campbell (ed.). *Man and Time*, Volume 3. Bolligen/Princeton.

Krupp, E.C. (1991). *Beyond the Blue Horizon: Myths and Legends of the Sun, Moon, Stars, and Planets*. Oxford University Press.

Kuan, S.H, K.H. Teng, and Aslaksen Helmer (1999–2000). *The Chinese Calendar of the Later Han Period*. Department of Mathematics, National University of Singapore.

Kuo, F.E. (2001). Coping with poverty: impacts of environment and attention in the inner city. *Environment & Behaviour* **33** (1), 5–34.

Kuo, Frances E., William C. Sullivan, Rebekah Levine Coley, and Lisette Brunson (December 1998). Fertile ground for community: inner-city neighborhood common spaces. *American Journal of Community Psychology* **26** (6), 823–51.

Lakoff, George, and Mark Johnson (1999). *Philosophy in the Flesh: The Embodied Mind and Its Challenge to Western Thought*. Basic Books.

Langworthy, Robert H. (undated). *Hot Area Topography*. Paper presented at the annual meeting of the Academy of Criminal Justice Sciences as part of the National Institute of Justice intramural research project 'A Multimethod Exploration of Crime Hot Spots'.

Lansing, J. Stephen (1991). *Priests and Programmers: Technologies of Power in the Engineered Landscape of Bali*. Princeton.

Lappé, Frances Moore, and Anna Lappé (2002). *Hope's Edge: The New Diet for a Small Planet*. J.P. Tarcher.

Lev, Esther (October–November 1998). A regional restoration grants program to promote preservation and enhancement of urban natural areas. *Urban Ecosystems* **2** (2–3), 103–11.

Lévi-Strauss, Claude (1979). *Myth and Meaning*. Schocken.

Liu Yanchi (1988). *The Essential Book of Traditional Chinese Medicine. Volume I: Theory*. Columbia.

Loewe, Michael (1995). *Divination, Mythology and Monarchy in Han China*. Cambridge.

Luck, Matthew, and Jianguo Wu (May 2002). A gradient analysis of urban landscape pattern: a case study from the Phoenix metropolitan region, Arizona, USA. *Landscape Ecology* **17** (4), 327–39.

Mackay, Charles (1841). *Extraordinary Popular Delusions and the Madness of Crowds*.

Major, John S. (1993). *Heaven and Earth in Early Han Thought: Chapters Three, Four, and Five of the Huainanzi*. SUNY.

Malmivuo, Jaakko, and Robert Plonsey (1995). *Bioelectromagnetism: Principles and Applications of Bioelectric and Biomagnetic Fields*. Oxford.

Marzluff, J.M., and K. Ewing (September 2001). Restoration of fragmented landscapes for the conservation of birds: a general framework and specific recommendations for urbanizing landscapes. *Restoration Ecology* **9** (3), 280–92.

May, Thomas Lee (May 1995). Temporal location theory, Kan Yu (Feng Shui)—an ancient Chinese theory on site location. *Paper Presented at the GeoInformatics 95 Conference, Hong Kong*.

May, Thomas Lee (1996). Kanyu—The book of change concept in environmental and architecture planning. *'Greening to the Blue' Conference*, Yale University School of Architecture.

McKibben, Bill (1989). *The End of Nature*. Random House.

McKibben, Bill (1995). *Hope, Human and Wild*. Little, Brown.

Medoff, Peter, and Holly Sklar (1994). *Streets of Hope: The Fall and Rise of an Urban Neighborhood*. South End Press.

Melamed, Samuel, Yitzhak Fried, and Paul Froom (2001). The interactive effect of chronic exposure to noise and job complexity on changes in blood pressure and job satisfaction: a longitudinal study of industrial employees. *Journal of Occupational Health Psychology* **6** (3), 182–95.

Mielczarek, Eugenie Vorburger, and Sharon Bertsch McGrayne (2000). *Iron, Nature's Universal Element: Why People Need Iron and Animals Make Magnets*. Rutgers.

Mildner, Gerald C.S., James G. Strathman, and Martha J. Bianco (December 1996). *Travel and Parking Behavior in the United States*. Center for Urban Studies, Discussion Paper No. DP96-7.

Miller, James R., and Richard J (April 2002). Hobbs. Conservation where people live and work. *Conservation Biology* **16** (2), 330–7.

Morrish, William R., and Catherine R. Brown (1994). *Planning to Stay*. Milkweed.

Morrison, Roy (1995). *Ecological Democracy*. South End Press.

Mörtberg, Ulla M (April 2001). Resident bird species in urban forest remnants; landscape and habitat perspectives. *Landscape Ecology* **16** (3), 193–203.

Mumford, Lewis (1961). *The City in History: Its Origins, Its Transformations, and Its Prospects*. Harvest/HBJ.

National Association of Home Builders (NAHB) Research Center (2001). *The Quiet Revolution: Building Greener, Building Better*. National Association of Home Builders.

National Wildlife Federation (2001). *Paving Paradise: Sprawl's Impact on Wildlife and Wild Places in California*. National Wildlife Federation.

Newman, Oscar (1996). *Creating Defensible Space*. US Department of Housing and Urban Development, Office of Policy Development and Research; Center for Urban Policy Research, Rutgers.

Ong, Han (2001). *Fixer Chao*. Farrar, Strans and Giroux.

Pankenier, David W. (2000–2001). Popular astrology and border affairs in early Imperial China: an archaeological confirmation. *Paper presented at INSAP III*.

Payne, Katy (1998). *Silent Thunder: In the Presence of Elephants*. Simon and Schuster.

Pielke Sr., R.A., G. Marland, R.A. Betts, T.N. Chase, J.L. Eastman, J.O. Niles, D. Niyogi, and S. Running (2002). The influence of land-use change and landscape dynamics on the climate system—relevance to climate change policy beyond the radiative effect of greenhouse gases. *Philosophical Transactions, Series A. Special Theme Issue* **360**, 1705–19.

Plunket, Emmeline (1997). *Calendars and Constellations of the Ancient World*. Senate.

Priestley, Thomas, and Gary W. Evans (March 1996). Resident perceptions of a nearby electric transmission line. *Journal of Environmental Psychology* **16** (1), 65–74.

Princen, Thomas, Michael Maniates, and Ken Conca (eds) (2002). *Confronting Consumption*. MIT Press.

Puth, Linda M., and Wilson, Karen A (February 2001). Boundaries and corridors as a continuum of ecological flow control: lessons from rivers and streams. *Conservation Biology* **15** (1), 21–30.

Rappenglück, Michael A. (September 1998). Palaeolithic shamanistic cosmography: how is the famous rock picture in the shaft of the Lascaux Grotto to be decoded? *Abstract from the ValCamonica Symposium*.

Rees et al. (2002). Analysis of magnetometer data using wavelet transforms. *Philosophical Transactions: Mathematical, Physical and Engineering Sciences. Proceedings of the Royal Society, Series A* **360** (1800). DOI: 10.1098/rsta.2002.1115.

Register, Richard (2002). *Ecocities: Building Cities in Balance with Nature*. Berkeley Hill Books.

Remen, Rachel Naomi (2000). *My Grandfather's Blessings*. Riverhead/ Penguin.

Rey, H.A. (1980). *The Stars: A New Way To See Them*. Houghton Mifflin.

Rich, Paul M., William A. Hetrick, and Shawn C. Saving (1994). Using viewshed models to calculate intercepted solar radiation: applications in ecology. *Proceedings of the ACSM/ASPRS Annual Convention and Exposition*, vol. 1, pp. 524–9.

Ritzer, George (1996). *The McDonaldization of Society*. Pine Forge Press.

Rosenfeld, Arthur, J. J. Romm, Hashem Akbari, Mel Pomerantz, and Haider Taha (1996). Policies to reduce heat islands: magnitudes of benefits and incentives to achieve them. In *Proceedings of the ACEEE 1996 Summer Study on Energy Efficiency in Buildings*, 25–31 August 1996. Washington, DC. American Council for an Energy-Efficient Economy. 1996. 9. 9.177–186. LBL-38679.

Rosenfeld Arthur H., Joseph J. Romm, Hashem Akbari, and Alan C. Lloyd (1997). Painting the town white—and green. *Technology Review* February/March.

Salafsky, N., H. Cauley, G. Balachander, B. Cordes, J. Parks, C. Margoluis, S. Bhatt, C. Encarnacion, D. Russell, and R. Margoluis (December 2002). A systematic test of an enterprise strategy for community-based biodiversity conservation. *Conservation Biology* **15** (6), 1585.

Samson, Paul, and Bertrand Charrier (August 1997). *International Freshwater Conflict: Issues and Prevention Strategies*. Green Cross International (http://www.gci.ch/GreenCrossPrograms/waterres/gcwater/ study.html).

Sauvajot, Raymond M., Marybeth Buechner, Denise A. Kamradt, and Christine M. Schonewald (December 1998). Patterns of human disturbance and response by small mammals and birds in chaparral near urban development. *Urban Ecosystems* **2** (4), 279–97.

Schecter, Bruce (14 October 2002). Massive balancing act pins down big G. *New Scientist* (http://www.newscientist.com).

Schiller, Andrew, and Sally P. Horn (1997). Wildlife conservation in urban greenways of the mid-southeastern United States. *Urban Ecosystems* **1** (2), 103–16.

Shapiro, Judith (2001). *Mao's War Against Nature: Politics and the Environment in Revolutionary China*. Cambridge.

Sharma, Mukul (10 June 2002). Variations in solar magnetic activity during the last 200,000 years: is there a Sun–climate connection? *Earth and Planetary Science Letters* **199** (3–4), 459–72.

Shen Yuzhi (1998). Chinese city planning thoughts noted by ancient books. *Paper presented at the Eighth International Conference on the History of Science in China.*

Sherr, Lynn (1997). *Tall Blondes: A Book about Giraffes.* Andrew McMeel.

Shibata, Seiji, and Naoto Suzuki (September 2002). Effects of the foliage plant on task performance and mood. *Journal of Environmental Psychology* **22** (3), 265–72.

Shiva, Vandana (1997). *Biopiracy: The Plunder of Nature and Knowledge.* South End Press.

Shiva, Vandana (2000). *Stolen Harvest: The Hijacking of the Global Food Supply.* South End Press.

Simons, Daniel J., and Christopher F. Chabris (1999). Gorillas in our midst: sustained inattentional blindness for dynamic events. *Perception* **28**, 1059–74.

Smith, Richard J. (1991). *Fortune-Tellers and Philosophers: Divination in Traditional Chinese Society.* Westview.

Smith, Richard J., and D.W.Y Kwok (eds) (1993). *Cosmology, Ontology, and Human Efficiacy: Essays in Chinese Thought.* University of Hawaii.

Soothill, William Edward (1951). *The Hall of Light: A Study of Early Chinese Kingship.* Lutterworth.

Steinhardt, Nancy Shatzman (1999). *Chinese Imperial City Planning.* University of Hawaii.

Strittholt, James R., and Domonick A (December 2002). Dellasala. Importance of roadless areas in biodiversity conservation in forested ecosystems: case study of the Klamath–Siskiyou ecoregion of the United States. *Conservation Biology* **15** (6), 1742.

Strong, Keith T., Julia L.R. Saba, Bernhard M. Haisch, and Joan T. Schmelz (eds) (1999). *The Many Faces of the Sun: A Summary of the Results from NASA's Solar Maximum Mission.* Springer.

Sun Xiaochun, and Jacob Kistemaker (1997). *The Chinese Sky During the Han: Constellating Stars and Society.* Brill.

Suzuki, David, and Amanda McConnell (1998). *The Sacred Balance: Rediscovering Our Place in Nature.* Prometheus.

Swart, J.A.A., H.J. van der Windt, and J. Keulartz (June 2001). Valuation of nature in conservation and restoration. *Restoration Ecology* **9** (2), 230–8.

Swenson, David X. (2002). *The Ouroboros Effect: The Revenge Effects of Unintended Consequences.* Last update January 2002. (http://www. css.edu/users/dswenson/web/REVENGE.HTM).

Ta La, Guo Zhizlong, Zhu Yanping, and Teng Minyu (September 2002). A progress report on the 1999–2000 seasons of the regional archaeological survey of the Chifeng Region, Inner Mongolia. *Abstracts of the 17th Indo-Pacific Prehistory Association Congress*, Taipei.

Tarrant, M.A., and H.K. Cordell (2002). Amenity values of public and private forests: examining the value-attitude relationship. *Environmental Management* **30** (5), 692–703.

Taylor, John S. (1983). *A Shelter Sketchbook: Timeless Building Solutions.* Chelsea Green.

Templer, John (1994). *The Staircase: Studies of Hazards, Falls, and Safer Design.* MIT Press.

Thomas, June Manning, John Metzger, Marsha Ritzdorf, Catherine Ross, and Bruce Stiftel (1997). *Race, Racism, and Race Relations: Linkage with Urban and Regional Planning Literature.* Michigan State University.

Thurston, George D. et al. (1997). Summertime haze air pollution and children with asthma. *American Journal of Respiratory and Critical Care Medicine* **155**, 654–60.

Tokar, Brian (1997). *Earth for Sale: Reclaiming Ecology in the Age of Corporate Greenwash.* South End Press.

Torrey, E. Fuller, and Judy Miller (2002). *The Invisible Plague: The Rise of Mental Illness from 1750 to the Present.* Rutgers.

Trinh Xuan Thuan (2001). *Chaos and Harmony.* Oxford.

Ulrich, Roger S. (1993). 'Biophilia, Biophobia, and Natural Landscapes.' In: Kellert, Stephen R., and Edward O. Wilson (eds). *The Biophilia Hypothesis.* Shearwater.

UNFPA (2002). *State of the World Population 2001.*

UNICEF, UNEP, and WHO (May 2002). *Children in the New Millennium: Environmental Impact on Health.* General Assembly Special Session on Children.

University Communications (26 February 2001). *Tongue Seen as Portal to the Brain.* University of Wisconsin—Madison (http://www.news.wisc.edu/).

Van Tonder, G., M.J. Lyons, and Y. Ejima (2002). Visual structure of a Japanese Zen garden. *Nature* **419**, 359.

Wackernagel, Mathis, Niels B. Schulz, Diana Deumling, Alejandro Callejas Linares, Martin Jenkins, Valerie Kapos, Chad Monfreda, Jonathan Loh, Norman Myers, Richard Norgaard, and Jørgen Randers (2002). Tracking the ecological overshoot of the human economy. *Proceedings of the National Academy of Sciences of the USA*, **99** (14), 9266–71, 9 July 2002.

Wallenius, Marjut (June 1999). Personal projects in everyday places: perceived supportiveness of the environment and psychological well-being. *Journal of Environmental Psychology* **19** (2), 131–43.

Walter, Katya (1996). *Tao of Chaos: Merging East and West.* Element.

Wang, Yeqiao, and Debra K. Moskovits (August 2002). Tracking fragmentation of natural communities and changes in land cover: applications of landsat data for conservation in an urban landscape (Chicago Wilderness). *Conservation Biology* **15** (4), 835–43.

Waterson, Roxana (1997). *The Living House: An Anthropology of Architecture in South-East Asia.* Whitney Library of Design.

Weathers, Kathleen C., Mary L. Cadenasso, and Steward T.A. Pickett (December 2002). Forest edges as nutrient and pollutant concentrators: potential synergisms between fragmentation, forest canopies, and the atmosphere. *Conservation Biology* **15** (6), 1506.

Wheatley, Paul (1971). *The Pivot of the Four Quarters.* Edinburgh.

Whitehouse, Sandra, James W. Varni, Michael Seid, Clare Cooper-Marcus, Mary Jane Ensengerg, Jenifer R. Jacobs, and Robyn. S. Mehlenbeck (September 2002). Evaluating a children's hospital garden environment: utilization and consumer satisfaction. *Journal of Environmental Psychology* **21** (3), 301–14.

Wichmann, Felix A., Lindsay T. Sharpe, and Karl R. Gegenfurtner (May 2002). The contributions of color to recognition memory for natural scenes. *Journal of Experimental Psychology: Learning, Memory, and Cognition* **28** (3), 509–20.

Williams, Richard J., Eric L. Berlow, Jennifer A. Dunne, Albert-László Barabási, and Neo D. Martinez (2002). Two degrees of separation in complex food webs. *Proceedings of the National Academy of Science of the USA*, Vol. 99, Issue 20, 12913–16.

Wilson, Edward O. (2002). *The Future of Life*. Knopf.

Wilson, Margaret A. (March 1996). The socialization of architectural preference. *Journal of Environmental Psychology* **16** (1), 33–44.

Wilson, Timothy D. (2002). *Strangers to Ourselves: Discovering the Adaptive Unconscious*. Belknap Press.

Wolf, Kathy (November 1998). *Urban Nature Benefits: Psycho-Social Dimensions of People and Plants*. Human Dimensions of the Urban Forest, Fact Sheet 1. Center for Urban Horticulture, University of Washington.

Wolf, Kathy (November 1998). *Trees in Business Districts: Positive Effects on Consumer Behavior!* Human Dimensions of the Urban Forest, Fact Sheet 5. Center for Urban Horticulture, University of Washington.

Wolf, Kathy (August 2000). *The Calming Effect of Green: Roadside Landscape and Driver Stress*. Human Dimensions of the Urban Forest, Fact Sheet 8. Center for Urban Horticulture, University of Washington.

Wolf, Kathy (August 2000). *Community Image: Roadside Settings and Public Perceptions*. Human Dimensions of the Urban Forest, Fact Sheet 10. Center for Urban Horticulture, University of Washington.

Woodwell, G.M. (2002). On purpose in science, conservation and government. The functional integrity of the earth is at issue not biodiversity. *Ambio* **31** (5), 432–6.

Wu, Jiahua (1995). *A Comparative Study of Landscape Aesthetics: Landscape Morphology*. Edwin Mellen.

Wu, Nelson (1968). *Chinese and Indian Architecture: The City of Man, the Mountain of God, and the Realm of the Immortals*. Studio Vista.

Yi-Fu Tuan (1974). *Topophilia: A Study of Environmental Perception, Attitudes, and Values*. Prentice-Hall.

Zhentao Xu, David W. Pankenier, and Yaotiao Jiang (2000). *East Asian Archaeoastronomy: Historical Records of Astronomical Observations of China, Japan and Korea*. Gordon and Breach.

Index